3rd Edition

Ventures 2

STUDENT'S BOOK

Gretchen Bitterlin ▪ Dennis Johnson ▪ Donna Price ▪ Sylvia Ramirez
K. Lynn Savage (Series Editor)

CAMBRIDGE
UNIVERSITY PRESS

CAMBRIDGE
UNIVERSITY PRESS

University Printing House, Cambridge CB2 8BS, United Kingdom

One Liberty Plaza, 20th Floor, New York, NY 10006, USA

477 Williamstown Road, Port Melbourne, VIC 3207, Australia

314–321, 3rd Floor, Plot 3, Splendor Forum, Jasola District Centre, New Delhi – 110025, India

79 Anson Road, #06–04/06, Singapore 079906

Cambridge University Press is part of the University of Cambridge.

It furthers the University's mission by disseminating knowledge in the pursuit of education, learning and research at the highest international levels of excellence.

www.cambridge.org
Information on this title: www.cambridge.org/9781108449564

First published 2008
Second edition 2014

20 19 18 17 16 15 14 13 12 11 10 9 8 7 6 5 4 3 2 1

Printed in Mexico by Editorial Impresora Apolo, S.A. de C.V.

A catalogue record for this publication is available from the British Library

ISBN 978-1-108-45000-3 Workbook
ISBN 978-1-108-44941-0 Online Workbook
ISBN 978-1-108-66609-1 Teacher's Edition
ISBN 978-1-108-44921-2 Class Audio CDs
ISBN 978-1-108-44912-0 Presentation Plus

Additional resources for this publication at www.cambridge.org/ventures

AUTHORS' ACKNOWLEDGMENTS

The authors would like to acknowledge and thank focus-group participants and reviewers for their insightful comments, as well as Cambridge University Press editorial, marketing, and production staffs, whose thorough research and attention to detail have resulted in a quality product.

The publishers would also like to extend their particular thanks to the following reviewers and consultants for their valuable insights and suggestions:

Barry Bakin, Instructional Technology, Los Angeles Unified School District, Los Angeles, CA;

Jim Brice, San Diego Community College District Continuing Education, San Diego, CA;

Diana Contreras, West Valley Occupational Center, Los Angeles, CA;

Druci J. Diaz, Hillsborough Country Public Schools, Tampa, FL;

Linda Foster, Instructor, Hillsborough County Schools Adult Education Department, Tampa, FL;

Margaret Geiger, M.Ed., Dallas, TX;

Ana L. Herrera, San Jacinto Adult Learning Center, El Paso, TX;

Cindi Hartmen, ESL Instructor, San Diego Continuing Education, San Diego, CA;

Patrick Jennings, Tomlinson Adult Learning Center, St. Petersburg, FL;

Lori Hess-Tolbert, Frisco, TX;

AnnMarie Kokash-Wood, Tomlinson Adult Learning Center, St. Petersburg, FL;

Linda P. Kozin, San Diego Continuing Ed, San Diego Community College District, San Diego, CA;

Caron Lieber, Palomar College, San Marcos, CA;

Reyna P. Lopez, Southwest College, Los Angeles, CA;

Rosemary Lubarov, Palo Alto Adult School, Palo Alto, CA;

Lori K. Markel, Plant City Adult and Community School, Plant City, FL;

Mary Spanarke, Center for Applied Linguistics / Washington English Center, Washington, DC;

Rosalie Tauscher, Fort Worth ISD Adult Ed, Fort Worth, TX;

Timothy Wahl, Abram Friedman Occupation Center, Los Angeles, CA;

Delia Watley, Irving ISD Adult Education and Literacy, Irving, TX;

Andrea V. White, Tarrant County College, Arlington, TX;

Sandra Wilson, Fort Worth Adult Education, Fort Worth, TX

SCOPE AND SEQUENCE

UNIT TITLE TOPIC	FUNCTIONS	LISTENING AND SPEAKING	VOCABULARY	GRAMMAR FOCUS
Welcome pages 2–5	■ Describing skills ■ Giving personal information	■ Talking about what classmates can do ■ Asking and answering questions about personal information	■ Review of regular and irregular verbs	■ Review of *be* – present and past ■ Review of present and past of regular and irregular verbs
Unit 1 **Personal information** pages 6–17 Topic: **Describing people**	■ Describing height, hair, and eyes ■ Describing clothing ■ Describing habitual actions ■ Describing actions in the present	■ Describing what people look like ■ Asking and describing what people are wearing ■ Asking and describing what people are doing at the present time ■ Asking and describing people's habitual actions	■ Accessories ■ Adjectives of size, color, and pattern	■ Adjective order ■ Present continuous vs. simple present ■ *and… too, and… either*, and *but*
Unit 2 **At school** pages 18–29 Topic: **School services**	■ Offering advice ■ Describing wants ■ Describing future plans	■ Asking and describing what people want and need ■ Asking about and describing future plans	■ Computer terms ■ Vocational courses	■ *Want* and *need* ■ The future with *will*, *be going to*, and the present continuous
Review: Units 1 and 2 pages 30–31		■ Understanding a narrative		
Unit 3 **Friends and family** pages 32–43 Topic: **Friends**	■ Describing past actions ■ Describing daily activities	■ Asking and answering questions about past actions ■ Asking and answering questions about daily habits	■ Parts of a car ■ Daily activities	■ Review of simple past with regular and irregular verbs ■ Simple present vs. simple past ■ Collocations with *make* and *do*; *play* and *go*
Unit 4 **Health** pages 44–55 Topic: **Accidents**	■ Identifying appropriate action after an accident ■ Asking for and giving advice ■ Expressing necessity ■ Showing understanding	■ Asking for and giving advice ■ Clarifying meaning	■ Health problems ■ Accidents ■ Terms on medicine packaging	■ *Should* ■ *Have to* + verb ■ *Must*, *must not*, *have to*, *not have to*
Review: Units 3 and 4 pages 56–57		■ Understanding a narrative		
Unit 5 **Around town** pages 58–69 Topic: **Transportation**	■ Identifying methods of transportation ■ Describing number of times ■ Describing length of time	■ Asking and answering questions about train, bus, and airline schedules ■ Asking and answering questions about personal transportation habits ■ Describing personal habits	■ Train station terms ■ Travel activities ■ Adverbs of frequency	■ *How often* and *How long* questions ■ Adverbs of frequency ■ The preposition *to* with movement

Student's Book 2

READING	WRITING	LIFE SKILLS	PRONUNCIATION
■ Reading a story about someone's family	■ Writing verb forms in past and present	■ Talking about your skills	■ Pronouncing key vocabulary
■ Reading an email about a family member ■ Scanning to find the answers to questions	■ Writing a descriptive paragraph about a classmate ■ Using a comma after time phrases at the beginning of a sentence	■ Reading an order form	■ Pronouncing key vocabulary
■ Reading a short essay on an application form ■ Skimming for the main idea	■ Writing an expository paragraph about goals ■ Using *First*, *Second*, and *Third* to organize ideas	■ Reading course descriptions ■ Setting short-term goals	■ Pronouncing key vocabulary
			■ Recognizing and pronouncing strong syllables
■ Reading a personal journal entry ■ Scanning for *First*, *Next*, and *Finally* to order events	■ Writing a personal journal entry about the events of a day ■ Using a comma after sequence words	■ Reading a chart about people's views	■ Pronouncing key vocabulary
■ Reading a warning label ■ Understanding a bulleted list	■ Filling out an accident report form ■ Using cursive writing for a signature	■ Reading medicine labels ■ Understanding a warning label	■ Pronouncing key vocabulary
			■ Recognizing and emphasizing important words
■ Reading a personal letter ■ Scanning for capital letters to determine names of cities and places	■ Writing an email about a trip ■ Spelling out hours and minutes from one to ten in writing	■ Reading a bus schedule ■ Reading a train schedule ■ Reading an airline schedule	■ Pronouncing key vocabulary

UNIT TITLE TOPIC	FUNCTIONS	LISTENING AND SPEAKING	VOCABULARY	GRAMMAR FOCUS
Unit 6 **Time** pages 70–81 Topic: **Time lines and major events**	■ Describing major events in the past ■ Inquiring about life events	■ Asking and answering questions about major life events in the past ■ Ordering events in the past	■ Life events ■ Time phrases	■ *When* questions and simple past ■ Time phrases ■ *Someone*, *some*, *anyone*, *everyone*, and *no one*
Review: Units 5 and 6 pages 82–83		■ Understanding a conversation		
Unit 7 **Shopping** pages 84–95 Topic: **Comparison shopping**	■ Comparing price and quality ■ Comparing two things ■ Comparing three or more things	■ Asking and answering questions to compare furniture, appliances, and stores	■ Furniture ■ Descriptive adjectives	■ Comparatives ■ Superlatives ■ *One*, *the other*, *some*, *the others*
Unit 8 **Work** pages 96–107 Topic: **Work history and job skills**	■ Identifying job duties ■ Describing work history	■ Asking and answering questions about completed actions ■ Connecting ideas	■ Hospital terms ■ Job duties	■ *What* and *Where* questions and simple past ■ Conjunctions *and*, *or*, *but* ■ Past and present ability with *could*, *couldn't*, *can*, and *can't*
Review: Units 7 and 8 pages 108–109		■ Understanding a narrative		
Unit 9 **Daily living** pages 110–121 Topic: **Solving common problems**	■ Asking for recommendations ■ Requesting help politely ■ Agreeing to a request ■ Refusing a request politely	■ Asking for and making recommendations ■ Explaining choices ■ Making polite requests ■ Agreeing to and refusing requests politely	■ Home problems ■ Descriptive adjectives	■ Requests with *Can*, *Could*, *Will*, *Would* ■ *Which* questions and simple present ■ *Let's* and *let's not*
Unit 10 **Free time** pages 122–133 Topic: **Special occasions**	■ Making offers politely ■ Responding to offers politely	■ Making offers politely ■ Responding to offers politely ■ Asking and answering questions involving direct and indirect objects	■ Celebrations ■ Party food ■ Gifts	■ *Would you like . . . ?* ■ Direct and indirect objects ■ *There is* / *there are* and *there was* / *there were*
Review: Units 9 and 10 pages 134–135		■ Understanding a conversation		

READING	WRITING	LIFE SKILLS	PRONUNCIATION
■ Reading a magazine interview ■ Skimming interview questions to determine the focus	■ Writing a narrative paragraph about important life events ■ Using a comma after a time phrase at the beginning of a sentence	■ Reading an application for a marriage license ■ Describing important life events in sequence	■ Pronouncing key vocabulary
			■ Pronouncing intonation in questions
■ Reading a short newspaper article ■ Guessing the meaning of new words from other words nearby	■ Writing a descriptive paragraph about a gift ■ Using *because* to answer *Why* and to give a reason	■ Reading a sales receipt	■ Pronouncing key vocabulary
■ Reading a letter of recommendation ■ Scanning text for names and dates	■ Writing a summary paragraph about employment history ■ Capitalizing the names of businesses	■ Reading a time sheet	■ Pronouncing key vocabulary
			■ Pronouncing the *-ed* ending in the simple past
■ Reading a notice on a notice board ■ Determining if new words are positive or negative in meaning	■ Writing a complaint email ■ Identifying the parts of a letter	■ Reading a customer invoice for service and repairs	■ Pronouncing key vocabulary
■ Reading a first-person narrative paragraph about a party ■ Looking for examples of the main idea while reading	■ Writing a thank-you note for a gift ■ Indenting paragraphs in an informal note	■ Reading a formal invitation to a party	■ Pronouncing key vocabulary
			■ Pronouncing the *-s* ending in the simple present

TO THE TEACHER

What is *Ventures*?

Ventures is a six-level, four-skills, standards-based, integrated-skills series that empowers students to achieve their academic and career goals.

- Aligned to the new NRS descriptors while covering key English Language Proficiency, College and Career Readiness Standards, and WIOA requirements.
- A wealth of resources provide instructors with the tools for any teaching situation, making *Ventures* the most complete program.
- Promotes 21st century learning complemented by a suite of technology tools.

How Does the Third Edition Meet Today's Adult Education Needs?

- The third edition is aligned to the NRS' interpretive, productive, and interactive outcomes at each level.
- To help students develop the skills they need to succeed in college and the workplace, *Ventures* 3rd Edition offers a dedicated College and Career Readiness Section (CCRS) with 10 worksheets at each level, from Level 1 to Transitions (pages 136–155).
- Audio tracks and grammar presentations linked to QR codes can be accessed using smartphones (see page x), promoting mobile learning.
- Problem-solving activities added to each unit cover critical thinking and soft skills key to workplace readiness.
- More rigorous grammar practice has been added to Lessons B and C, and more evidence-based reading practice has been added to Lesson D.

What are the *Ventures* components?

Student's Book

Each of the core **Student's Books** contains ten topic-focused units, with five review units. The main units feature six skill-focused lessons.

- **Self-contained lessons** are perfectly paced for one-hour classes. For classes longer than 1 hour, additional resources are available via the Workbook and Online Teacher's Resources.
- **Review units** recycle and reinforce the listening, vocabulary, and grammar skills developed in the two prior units and include a pronunciation activity.

Teacher's Edition

The interleaved **Teacher's Edition** includes easy-to-follow lesson plans for every unit.

- Teaching tips address common problem areas for students and additional suggestions for expansion activities and building community.
- Additional practice material across all *Ventures* components is clearly organized in the *More Ventures* chart at the end of each lesson.
- Multiple opportunities for assessment such as unit, mid-term, and final tests are available in the Teacher's Edition. Customizable tests and test audio are also available online (www.cambridge.org/ventures/resources/).

Online Teacher's Resources www.cambridge.org/ventures/resources/

Ventures Online Teacher's Resources offer hundreds of additional worksheets and classroom materials including:

- *A placement test* that helps accurately identify the appropriate level of *Ventures* for each student.
- *Career and Educational Pathways Worksheets* help students meet their post-exit employment goals.
- *Collaborative Worksheets* for each lesson develop cooperative learning and community building within the classroom.
- *Writing Worksheets* that help literacy-level students recognize shapes and write letters and numbers, while alphabet and number cards promote partner and group work.
- *Picture dictionary cards and Worksheets* that reinforce vocabulary learned in Levels Basic, 1, and 2.
- *Multilevel Worksheets* that are designed for use in multilevel classrooms and in leveled classes where the proficiency level of students differs.
- *Self-assessments* give students an opportunity to reflect on their learning. They support learner persistence and help determine whether students are ready for the unit test.

Workbook

The **Workbook** provides two pages of activities for each lesson in the Student's Book.

- If used in class, the Workbook can extend classroom instructional time by 30 minutes per lesson.
- The exercises are designed so learners can complete them in class or independently. Students can check their answers with the answer key in the back of the Workbook. Workbook exercises can be assigned in class, for homework, or as student support when a class is missed.
- Grammar charts at the back of the Workbook allow students to use the Workbook for self-study.

Online Workbooks

The self-grading **Online Workbooks** offer programs the flexibility of introducing blended learning.

- In addition to the same high-quality practice opportunities in the print workbooks, the online workbooks provide students instant feedback.
- Teachers and programs can track student progress and time on task.

Presentation Plus
www.esource.cambridge.org

Presentation Plus allows teachers to digitally project the contents of the Student's Books in front of the class for a livelier, interactive classroom. It is a complete solution for teachers because it includes the Class audio, answer keys, and the Ventures Arcade. Contact your Cambridge ESL Specialist (www.cambridge.org/cambridgeenglish/contact) to find out how to access it.

Ventures Arcade
www.cambridge.org/venturesarcade/

The Arcade is a free website where students can find additional practice for the listening, vocabulary, and grammar found in the Student's Books. There is also a Citizenship section that includes questions on civics, history, government, and the N-400 application.

Unit organization

LESSON A Listening focuses students on the unit topic. The initial exercise, ***Before you listen***, creates student interest with visuals that help the teacher assess what learners already know and serves as a prompt for the unit's key vocabulary. Next is ***Listen***, which is based on conversations. Students relate vocabulary to meaning and relate the spoken and written forms of new theme-related vocabulary. ***After you listen*** concludes the lesson by practicing language related to the theme in a communicative activity, either orally with a partner or individually in a writing activity.

LESSONS B AND C focus on grammar. The lessons move from a ***Grammar focus*** that presents the grammar point in chart form; to ***Practice*** exercises that check comprehension of the grammar point and provide guided practice; and, finally, to ***Communicate*** exercises that guide learners as they generate original answers and conversations. These lessons often include a *Culture note*, which provides information directly related to the conversation practice (such as the use of titles with last names) or a *Useful language* note, which introduces useful expressions.

LESSON D Reading develops reading skills and expands vocabulary. The lesson opens with a ***Before you read*** exercise, designed to activate prior knowledge and encourage learners to make predictions. A *Reading tip*, which focuses on a specific reading skill, accompanies the ***Read*** exercise. The reading section of the lesson concludes with ***After you read*** exercises that check comprehension. In Levels Basic, 1, and 2, the vocabulary expansion portion of the lesson is a ***Picture dictionary***. It includes a *word bank*, pictures to identify, and a conversation for practicing the new words. The words expand vocabulary related to the unit topic. In Books 3 and 4, the vocabulary expansion portion of the lesson uses new vocabulary from the reading to build skills such as recognizing word families, selecting definitions based on the context of the reading, and using clues in the reading to guess meaning.

LESSON E Writing provides practice with process writing within the context of the unit. ***Before you write*** exercises provide warm-up activities to activate the language needed for the writing assignment, followed by one or more exercises that provide a model for students to follow when they write. A *Writing tip* presents information about punctuation or paragraph organization directly related to the writing assignment. The ***Write*** exercise sets goals for the student writing. In the ***After you write*** exercise, students share with a partner.

LESSON F Another view brings the unit together with opportunities to review lesson content. ***Life-skills reading*** develops the scanning and skimming skills used with documents such as forms, charts, schedules, announcements, and ads. Multiple-choice questions (modeled on CASAS[1] and BEST[2]) develop test-taking skills. **Solve the problem** focuses on critical thinking, soft-skills, and workplace development. In Levels 1–4, ***Grammar connections*** contrasts grammar points and includes guided practice and communicative activities.

---

1 The Comprehensive Adult Student Assessment System. For more information, see www.casas.org.

2 The Basic English Skills Test. For more information, see www.cal.org/BEST.

UNIT TOUR

The Most Complete Course for Student Success

- Helps students develop the skills needed to be college and career ready and function successfully in their community
- Covers key NRS and WIOA requirements
- Aligned with the English Language Proficiency (ELP) and College and Career Readiness (CCR) standards

The Big Picture

- Introduces the unit topic and creates an opportunity for classroom discussion.
- Activates students' prior knowledge and previews the unit vocabulary.

Unit Goals

Introduces the competencies students will learn.

UNIT 8 WORK

Lesson A Listening

1 Before you listen

A Look at the picture. What do you see?

B Point to: ■ a lab ■ linens ■ a patient ■ a walker supplies ■ co-workers ■ an orderly ■ a wheelchair

C Look at these people. What are they doing?

UNIT GOALS

Describe job duties **Describe** past activities

Interpret information on a weekly time sheet

2 Listen

A **Listen.** What is Marco talking about? Write the letter of the conversation.

1. ___ 2. ___ 3. ___

CD2, Track 15

B **Listen again.** Write *T* (true) or *F* (false).

CD2, Track 16

Conversation A

1. Marco picked up X-rays this morning. *T*
2. Marco delivered linens to the third floor. ___
3. Marco needs to prepare rooms on the second floor. ___

Conversation B

4. John is tired. ___
5. Marco worked the night shift. ___
6. Marco wants to go back to school. ___

Conversation C

7. Suzanne works in Human Resources. ___
8. Marco wants to be a nurse. ___
9. Marco wants to work full-time. ___

Listen again. Check your answers. Correct the false statements.

CULTURE NOTE

People who work at night work the night shift.

3 After you listen

Talk with a partner. Ask and answer the questions.

1. Do you have a job? What do you do?
2. Did you have a job before? What did you do?
3. What job do you want in the future?

Listen for and identify job duties UNIT 8 97

How to use a QR code

- Open the camera on your smartphone.
- Point it at the QR code.
- The camera will automatically scan the code. If not, press the button to take a picture.

* Not all cameras automatically scan QR codes. You may need to download a QR code reader. Search "QR free" and download an app.

3 Easy Ways to Access Audio

- Scan QR codes
- Download from *Ventures* Online Resources: www.cambridge.org/ventures/audio/
- Play from Class audio CDs

Every unit has two grammar lessons taught using the same format.

Grammar Chart

- Presents and practices the grammar point.
- Extra grammar charts online can be used for reference and give additional support.

Grammar Presentation

Animated presentations to watch on mobile devices using QR codes allow for self-directed learning and develop digital literacy.

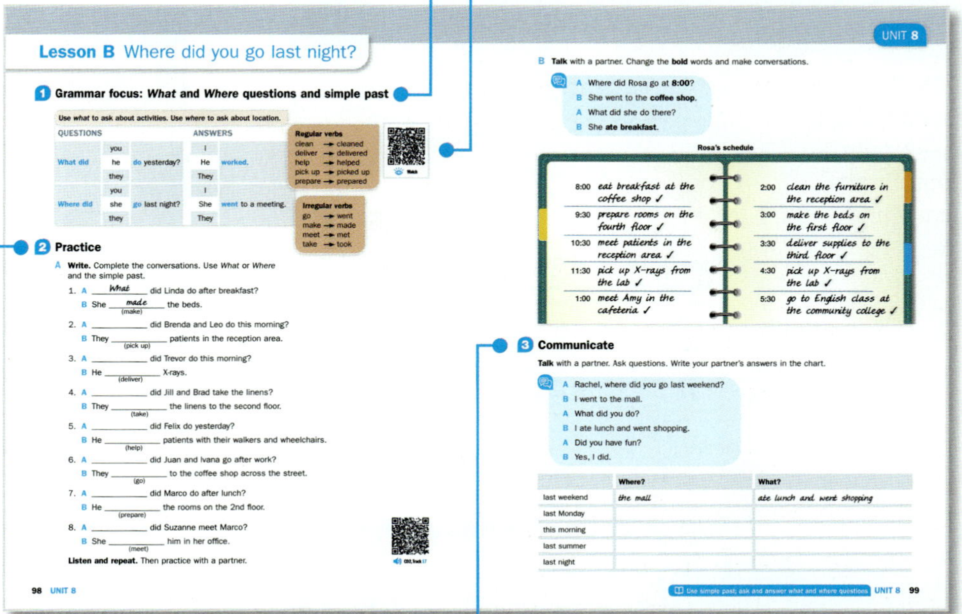
Lesson B Where did you go last night?

UNIT 8

1 Grammar focus: *What* and *Where* questions and simple past

Use *what* to ask about activities. Use *where* to ask about location.

QUESTIONS			ANSWERS		
What did	you / he / they	do yesterday?	I / He / They	worked.	
Where did	you / she / they	go last night?	I / She / They	went to a meeting.	

Regular verbs: clean → cleaned, deliver → delivered, help → helped, pick up → picked up, prepare → prepared

Irregular verbs: go → went, make → made, meet → met, take → took

2 Practice

A **Write.** Complete the conversations. Use *What* or *Where* and the simple past.

1. A *What* did Linda do after breakfast?
   B She *made* (make) the beds.
2. A ______ did Brenda and Leo do this morning?
   B They ______ (pick up) patients in the reception area.
3. A ______ did Trevor do this morning?
   B He ______ (deliver) X-rays.
4. A ______ did Jill and Brad take the linens?
   B They ______ (take) the linens to the second floor.
5. A ______ did Felix do yesterday?
   B He ______ (help) patients with their walkers and wheelchairs.
6. A ______ did Juan and Ivana go after work?
   B They ______ (go) to the coffee shop across the street.
7. A ______ did Marco do after lunch?
   B He ______ (prepare) the rooms on the 2nd floor.
8. A ______ did Suzanne meet Marco?
   B She ______ (meet) him in her office.

Listen and repeat. Then practice with a partner.

B **Talk** with a partner. Change the **bold** words and make conversations.

A Where did Rosa go at **8:00**?
B She went to the **coffee shop**.
A What did she do there?
B She **ate breakfast**.

Rosa's schedule

8:00	eat breakfast at the coffee shop ✓	2:00	clean the furniture in the reception area ✓
9:30	prepare rooms on the fourth floor ✓	3:00	make the beds on the first floor ✓
10:30	meet patients in the reception area ✓	3:30	deliver supplies to the third floor ✓
11:30	pick up X-rays from the lab ✓	4:30	pick up X-rays from the lab ✓
1:00	meet Amy in the cafeteria ✓	5:30	go to English class at the community college ✓

3 Communicate

Talk with a partner. Ask questions. Write your partner's answers in the chart.

A Rachel, where did you go last weekend?
B I went to the mall.
A What did you do?
B I ate lunch and went shopping.
A Did you have fun?
B Yes, I did.

	Where?	What?
last weekend	the mall	ate lunch and went shopping
last Monday		
this morning		
last summer		
last night		

98 UNIT 8

Use simple past; ask and answer *what* and *where* questions UNIT 8 99

Additional Grammar Activities

Ensures students have the chance to practice more grammar to meet the rigor of CCRS.

Natural Progression

Moves from controlled to communicative activities for students to ask and answer questions about familiar text, topics, and experiences.

Real-life Practice

Engages students and provides meaningful application of the grammar.

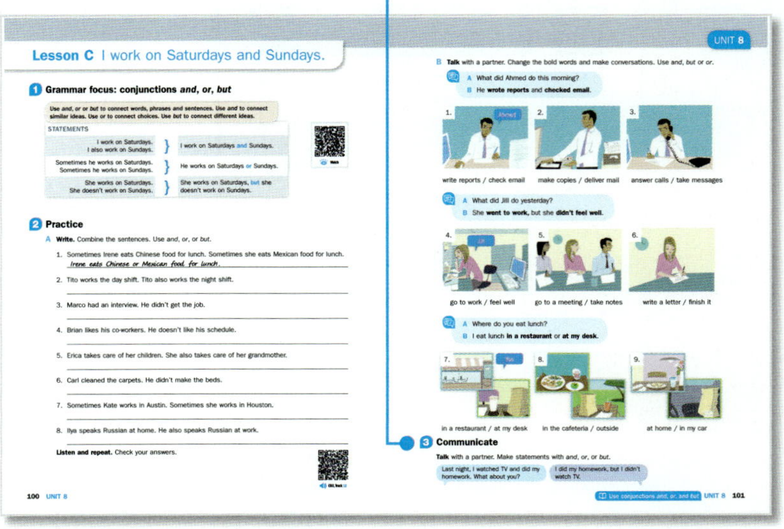
Lesson C I work on Saturdays and Sundays.

UNIT 8

1 Grammar focus: conjunctions *and*, *or*, *but*

2 Practice

A **Write.** Combine the sentences. Use *and*, *or*, or *but*.

1. Sometimes Irene eats Chinese food for lunch. Sometimes she eats Mexican food for lunch.
   Irene eats Chinese or Mexican food for lunch.
2. Tito works the day shift. Tito also works the night shift.
3. Marco had an interview. He didn't get the job.
4. Brian likes his co-workers. He doesn't like his schedule.
5. Erica takes care of her children. She also takes care of her grandmother.
6. Carl cleaned the carpets. He didn't make the beds.
7. Sometimes Kate works in Austin. Sometimes she works in Houston.
8. Ilya speaks Russian at home. He also speaks Russian at work.

Listen and repeat. Check your answers.

B **Talk** with a partner. Change the bold words and make conversations. Use *and*, *but* or *or*.

A What did Ahmed do this morning?
B He **wrote reports** and **checked email**.

write reports / check email — make copies / deliver mail — answer calls / take messages

A What did Jill do yesterday?
B She **went to work**, but she **didn't feel well**.

go to work / feel well — go to a meeting / take notes — write a letter / finish it

A Where do you eat lunch?
B I eat lunch **in a restaurant** or **at my desk**.

in a restaurant / at my desk — in the cafeteria / outside — at home / in my car

3 Communicate

Talk with a partner. Make statements with *and*, *or*, *but*.

Last night, I watched TV and did my homework. What about you?
I did my homework, but I didn't watch TV.

100 UNIT 8

Use conjunctions *and*, *or*, and *but* UNIT 8 101

Reading

- Uses a 3-step reading approach to highlight the skills and strategies students need to succeed.
- Combines reading with writing and listening practice for an integrated approach to ensure better comprehension.
- Brings text complexity into the classroom to help students read independently and proficiently.

Picture dictionary

Expands unit vocabulary and practices pronunciation for deeper understanding of the topic.

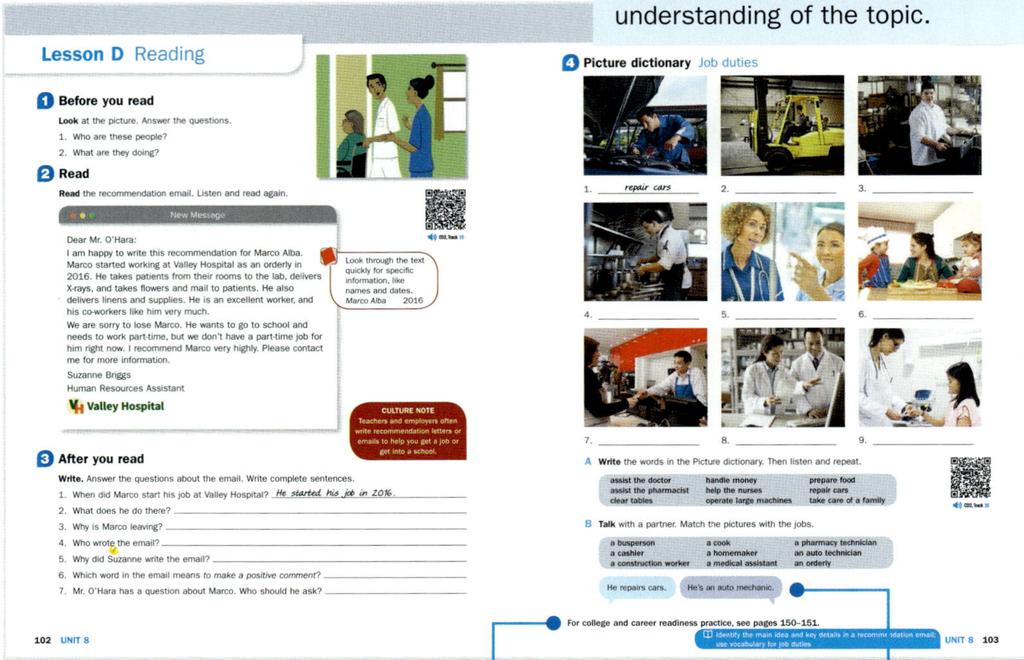

Lesson D Reading

1 Before you read

Look at the picture. Answer the questions.

1. Who are these people?
2. What are they doing?

2 Read

Read the recommendation email. Listen and read again.

New Message

Dear Mr. O'Hara:

I am happy to write this recommendation for Marco Alba. Marco started working at Valley Hospital as an orderly in 2016. He takes patients from their rooms to the lab, delivers X-rays, and takes flowers and mail to patients. He also delivers linens and supplies. He is an excellent worker, and his co-workers like him very much.

We are sorry to lose Marco. He wants to go to school and needs to work part-time, but we don't have a part-time job for him right now. I recommend Marco very highly. Please contact me for more information.

Suzanne Briggs
Human Resources Assistant
Valley Hospital

Look through the text quickly for specific information, like names and dates. *Marco Alba* 2016

CULTURE NOTE
Teachers and employers often write recommendation letters or emails to help you get a job or get into a school.

3 After you read

Write. Answer the questions about the email. Write complete sentences.

1. When did Marco start his job at Valley Hospital? *He started his job in 2016.*
2. What does he do there?
3. Why is Marco leaving?
4. Who wrote the email?
5. Why did Suzanne write the email?
6. Which word in the email means *to make a positive comment*?
7. Mr. O'Hara has a question about Marco. Who should he ask?

102 UNIT 8

4 Picture dictionary Job duties

1. *repair cars* 2. 3. 4. 5. 6. 7. 8. 9.

A **Write** the words in the Picture dictionary. Then listen and repeat.

assist the doctor	handle money	prepare food
assist the pharmacist	help the nurses	repair cars
clear tables	operate large machines	take care of a family

B **Talk** with a partner. Match the pictures with the jobs.

a busperson	a cook	a pharmacy technician
a cashier	a homemaker	an auto technician
a construction worker	a medical assistant	an orderly

He repairs cars. He's an auto mechanic.

For college and career readiness practice, see pages 150–151.

Identify the main idea and key details in a recommendation email. Use vocabulary for job duties

UNIT 8 103

College & Career Readiness Section

Builds critical-thinking skills and uses informative texts to help master the more complex CCR standards.

Speaking Practice

Helps students internalize the vocabulary and relate it to their lives.

Writing

- Helps students develop a robust process-writing approach.
- Supports students to meet the challenges of work and the classroom through academic and purposeful writing practice.

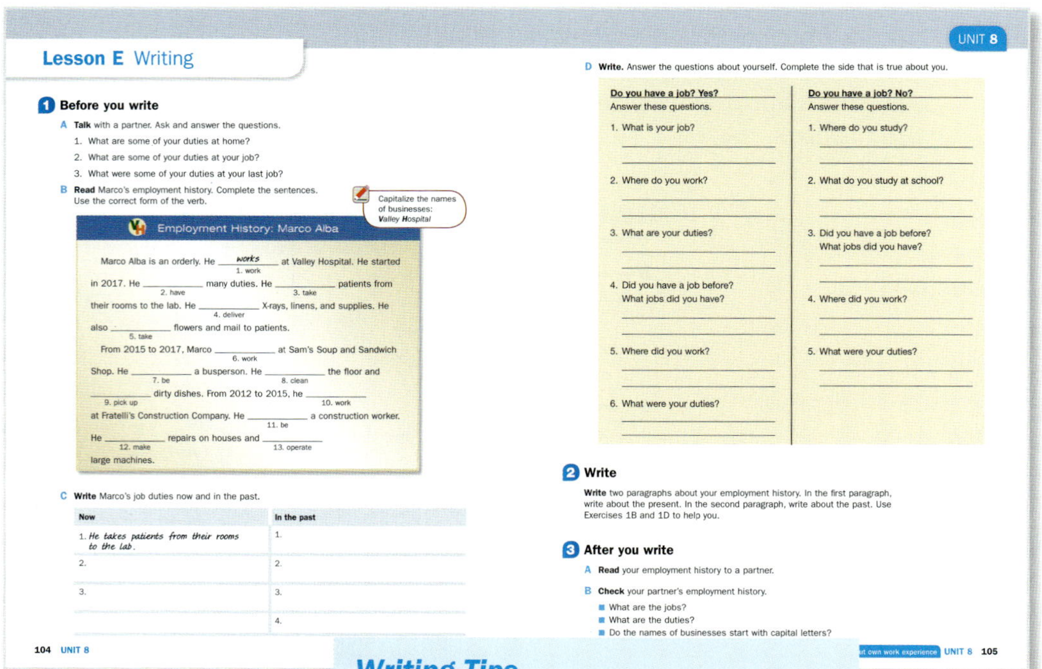

Lesson E Writing

1 Before you write

A **Talk** with a partner. Ask and answer the questions.

1. What are some of your duties at home?
2. What are some of your duties at your job?
3. What were some of your duties at your last job?

B **Read** Marco's employment history. Complete the sentences. Use the correct form of the verb.

Capitalize the names of businesses: *Valley Hospital*

Employment History: Marco Alba

Marco Alba is an orderly. He *works* (1. work) at Valley Hospital. He started in 2017. He ______ (2. have) many duties. He ______ (3. take) patients from their rooms to the lab. He ______ (4. deliver) X-rays, linens, and supplies. He also ______ (5. take) flowers and mail to patients.

From 2015 to 2017, Marco ______ (6. work) at Sam's Soup and Sandwich Shop. He ______ (7. be) a busperson. He ______ (8. clean) the floor and ______ (9. pick up) dirty dishes. From 2012 to 2015, he ______ (10. work) at Fratelli's Construction Company. He ______ (11. be) a construction worker. He ______ (12. make) repairs on houses and ______ (13. operate) large machines.

C **Write** Marco's job duties now and in the past.

Now	In the past
1. *He takes patients from their rooms to the lab.*	1.
2.	2.
3.	3.
	4.

104 UNIT 8

UNIT 8

D **Write.** Answer the questions about yourself. Complete the side that is true about you.

Do you have a job? Yes? Answer these questions.	Do you have a job? No? Answer these questions.
1. What is your job?	1. Where do you study?
2. Where do you work?	2. What do you study at school?
3. What are your duties?	3. Did you have a job before? What jobs did you have?
4. Did you have a job before? What jobs did you have?	4. Where did you work?
5. Where did you work?	5. What were your duties?
6. What were your duties?	

2 Write

Write two paragraphs about your employment history. In the first paragraph, write about the present. In the second paragraph, write about the past. Use Exercises 1B and 1D to help you.

3 After you write

A **Read** your employment history to a partner.

B **Check** your partner's employment history.

- What are the jobs?
- What are the duties?
- Do the names of businesses start with capital letters?

UNIT 8 105

Writing Tips

Gives students confidence in writing with easy-to-follow writing tips and strategies.

Document Literacy

Builds real-life skills through explicit practice using authentic document types.

Grammar connections

Contrasts two grammar forms in a communicative way to help with grammar accuracy.

Test-taking Skills

Prepares students for standarized tests like the CASAS by familiarizing them with bubble answer format.

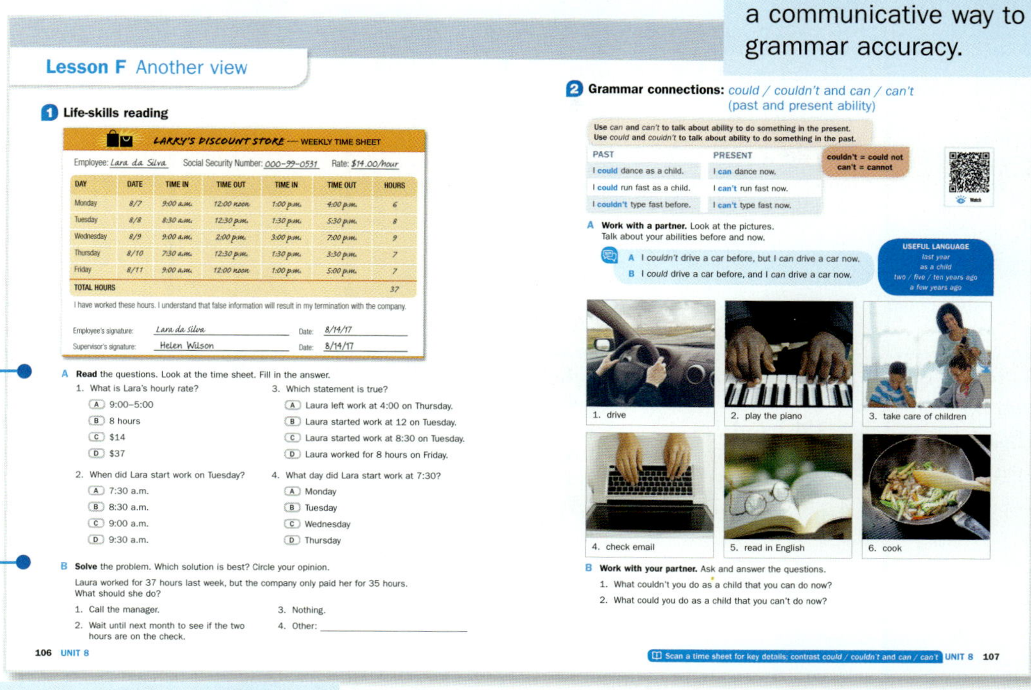

Problem-solving Activity

Covers critical thinking and soft skills – crucial for workplace readiness – and helps students meet WIOA requirements.

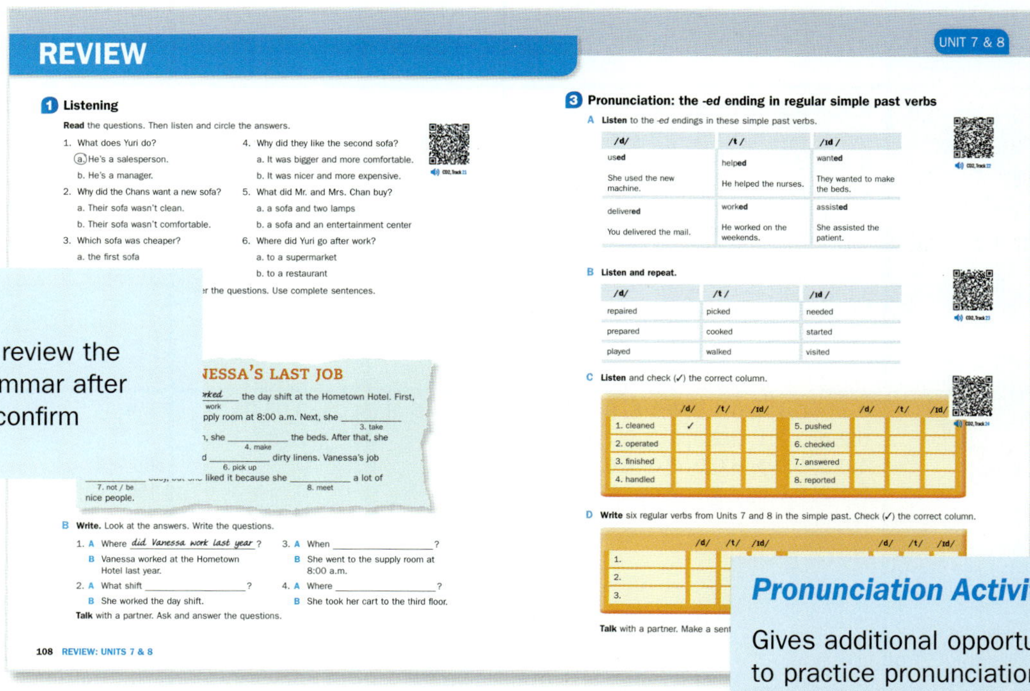

Review Pages

Allows students to review the vocabulary and grammar after every two units to confirm retention.

Pronunciation Activities

Gives additional opportunities to practice pronunciation and promotes spoken fluency.

CORRELATIONS

UNIT	CASAS Competencies	Florida Adult ESOL Low Beginning	LAUSD ESL Beginning Low Competencies
Unit 1 **Personal information** Pages 6–17	0.1.2, 0.1.4, 0.1.5, 0.1.6, 0.2.1, 0.2.3, 0.2.4, 1.1.6, 1.1.9, 1.2.1, 1.2.5, 1.3.1, 1.3.3, 1.3.4, 1.3.9, 1.6.4, 2.4.2, 2.6.1, 4.8.1, 4.8.2, 4.8.3, 6.0.2, 7.2.1, 7.4.7, 7.5.1, 8.1.2, 8.1.4	3.01.01, 3.01.03, 3.03.16, 3.04.01, 3.04.06, 3.04.08, 3.04.09	I. 1, 3, 4, 5, 6 II. 7a, 11e III. 14 IV. 27 VIII. 62
Unit 2 **At school** Pages 18–29	0.1.2, 0.1.4, 0.1.5, 0.2.1, 0.2.4, 1.2.1, 1.9.6, 2.3.2, 2.5.5, 4.1.4, 4.1.6, 4.1.7, 4.1.8, 4.1.9, 4.4.2, 4.4.5, 4.8.1, 4.8.2, 7.1.1, 7.1.4, 7.2.2, 7.2.6, 7.3.1, 7.3.2, 7.3.4, 7.4.2, 7.4.7, 7.4.8, 7.5.1, 7.5.7, 8.3.2	3.03.01, 3.03.05, 3.03.13, 3.03.14	I. 5 II. 7a III. 12, 14, 15 VIII. 59
Unit 3 **Friends and family** Pages 32–43	0.1.2, 0.1.4, 0.1.5, 0.2.1, 0.2.4, 1.2.1, 1.2.2, 1.2.4, 1.2.5, 1.5.2, 2.1.4, 2.6.1, 4.8.1, 4.8.2, 4.8.4, 6.0.1, 6.0.2, 6.0.3, 6.0.4, 6.1.1, 6.1.3, 6.2.3, 6.5.1, 6.6.6, 7.1.4, 7.2.1, 7.2.7, 7.3.2, 7.4.2, 7.4.3, 7.4.7, 7.5.1, 8.1.2, 8.2.1, 8.2.2, 8.2.3, 8.2.4	3.01.03, 3.01.08, 3.02.02, 3.02.08, 3.03.16, 3.04.01, 3.04.06, 3.05.04	II. 71 III. 17a IV. 32 VIII. 59, 62
Unit 4 **Health** Pages 44–55	0.1.2, 0.1.4, 0.1.5, 0.2.1, 1.2.5, 3.1.1, 3.2.1, 3.3.1, 3.3.2, 3.4.1, 3.4.2, 3.4.3, 3.5.9, 4.3.3, 4.8.1, 7.1.4, 7.2.1, 7.3.2, 7.4.2, 7.4.7	3.05.01, 3.05.04, 3.07.01	II. 7b III. 17a VI. 45, 47, 49 VII. 57
Unit 5 **Around town** Pages 58–69	0.1.2, 0.1.4, 0.1.5, 0.1.6, 0.2.1, 0.2.4, 2.2.1, 2.2.3, 2.2.4, 2.3.1, 4.8.1, 6.0.1, 6.0.2, 6.0.3, 6.0.4, 6.1.2, 6.6.6, 7.1.1, 7.4.2, 7.4.7	3.03.16, 3.04.01, 3.06.01	I. 4 II. 7b, 8c III. 23b VIII. 62

For more details and correlations to other state standards, go to: www.cambridge.org/ventures/correlations

NRS Educational Functioning Level Descriptors	English Language Proficiency and College and Career Readiness Standards
Interpretive ■ Identify the main topic and key details in conversations about what people look like. ■ Identify the main topic and key details in a reading about a family member. ■ Determine the meaning of common words and phrases related to describing people. ■ Determine the main idea and key details on an order form. **Productive** ■ Compose a short paragraph about a classmate ■ Use *adjective order*, *and...too*, *and...either*, and *but*, and compare *present continuous* with *simple present*. ■ Deliver a short oral presentation on findings from the Internet about an online clothing store. **Interactive** ■ Participate in conversations about describing people. ■ Gather and record information from the Internet about an online clothing store.	ELP Standards 1–10 Reading Anchors 1, 2, 4, 5, 7, 9, 10 Speaking & Listening Anchors 1, 2, 3, 4, 6
Interpretive ■ Identify the main topic and key details in conversations about what people want and need. ■ Identify the main topic and key details in an application form. ■ Determine the meaning of common words and phrases related to school services. ■ Determine the main idea and key details in a course description. **Productive** ■ Compose a short expository paragraph about goals. ■ Use *want* and *need* and the *future* with *will*, *be going to*, and the *present continuous*. ■ Use *first*, *second* and *third* person to organize ideas. ■ Deliver a short oral presentation on findings from interviews about three jobs. **Interactive** ■ Participate in conversations about school services. ■ Gather and record information from interviews about three jobs.	ELP Standards 1–10 Reading Anchors 1, 2, 3, 4, 5, 7, 9, 10 Speaking & Listening Anchors 1, 2, 3, 4, 6
Interpretive ■ Identify the main topic and key details in conversations about past actions and daily habits. ■ Identify the main topic and key details in a personal journal entry. ■ Determine the meaning of common words and phrases related to friends. ■ Determine the main idea and key details on a cell phone calling-plan brochure. **Productive** ■ Compose a short personal journal entry about the events of a day. ■ Use *collocations* with *make* and *do*; *play and go*, and review *simple past* with *regular* and *irregular verbs*. ■ Use words like *first*, *next*, and *finally* to tell the order of events. ■ Deliver a short oral presentation on findings from Internet about weekend activities in your city. **Interactive** ■ Participate in conversations about friends. ■ Gather and record information from the Internet about weekend activities in your city.	ELP Standards 1–10 Reading Anchors 1, 2, 4, 5, 7, 9, 10 Speaking & Listening Anchors 1, 2, 3, 4, 6
Interpretive ■ Identify the main topic and key details in conversations about asking for and giving advice. ■ Identify the main topic and key details in a warning label. ■ Determine the meaning of common words and phrases related to accidents. ■ Determine the main idea and key details on a medicine label. **Productive** ■ Fill out an accident report form. ■ Use *should*, *have to + verb*, *must*, *must not*, *have to*, and *not have to*. ■ Deliver a short oral presentation on findings from medication from your medicine cabinet. **Interactive** ■ Participate in conversations about accidents. ■ Gather and record information from your medicine cabinet.	ELP Standards 1–10 Reading Anchors 1, 2, 4, 5, 7, 9, 10 Speaking & Listening Anchors 1, 2, 3, 4, 6
Interpretive ■ Identify the main topic and key details in conversations about transportation schedules and personal transportation habits. ■ Identify the main topic and key details in a personal letter. ■ Determine the meaning of common words and phrases related to transportation. ■ Determine the main idea and key details on a bus, train, and airline schedule. **Productive** ■ Compose a short personal letter about a trip. ■ Use *how long/how often* questions, *adverbs of frequency*, and *prepositions*. ■ Deliver a short oral presentation on findings from the Internet about a trip you planned. **Interactive** ■ Participate in conversations about transportation. ■ Gather and record information from the Internet to plan a trip.	ELP Standards 1–10 Reading Anchors 1, 2, 4, 5, 7, 9, 10 Speaking & Listening Anchors 1, 2, 3, 4, 6

UNIT	CASAS Competencies	Florida Adult ESOL Low Beginning	LAUSD ESL Beginning Low Competencies
Unit 6 **Time** Pages 70–81	0.1.2, 0.1.4, 0.1.5, 0.2.1, 0.2.3, 0.2.4, 2.3.1, 2.3.2, 2.7.2, 4.8.1, 5.3.1, 5.3.6, 6.0.1, 7.1.1, 7.2.1, 7.2.4, 7.2.7, 7.4.2, 7.4.3, 7.4.7, 7.4.8, 7.5.1	3.03.01, 3.03.09, 3.04.01	I. 4, 5 II. 7a III. 5 VIII. 62
Unit 7 **Shopping** Pages 84–95	0.1.2, 0.1.4, 0.1.5, 0.2.1, 1.1.6, 1.2.1, 1.2.2, 1.2.6, 1.2.7, 1.4.1, 1.6.3, 4.8.1, 6.0.1, 6.0.2, 7.1.1, 7.2.3, 7.4.2, 7.4.7, 7.5.1, 8.1.4	3.03.01, 3.04.01, 3.04.06, 3.06.03	III. 23b IV. 27, 30, 32 VIII. 62
Unit 8 **Work** Pages 96–107	0.1.2, 0.1.4, 0.1.5, 0.2.1, 1.1.6, 2.3.1, 2.3.2, 4.1.2, 4.1.6, 4.1.8, 4.2.1, 4.4.3, 4.5.1, 4.8.1, 4.8.2, 6.0.1, 7.1.1, 7.1.4, 7.2.1, 7.2.3, 7.4.7, 7.5.1	3.01.03, 3.03.01, 3.03.13, 3.03.14, 3.03.16	I. 5 II. 7a, 7b, 8a, 8b, 22 III. 25 VIII. 62
Unit 9 **Daily living** Pages 110–121	0.1.2, 0.1.4, 0.1.5, 0.2.1, 0.2.3, 1.1.6, 1.4.1, 1.4.5, 1.4.7, 1.5.2, 1.6.3, 1.7.4, 1.7.5, 4.1.8, 4.8.1, 4.8.6, 6.0.1, 7.1.1, 7.1.2, 7.2.1, 7.2.2, 7.3.2, 7.3.4, 7.4.2, 7.4.7, 7.5.1, 7.5.6, 8.1.4, 8.2.6, 8.3.1, 8.3.2	3.01.02, 3.04.05, 3.04.06	II. 7a, 7b, 9b, 9c, 10a III. 25 V. 27, 32, 39
Unit 10 **Free time** Pages 122–133	0.1.2, 0.1.4, 0.1.5, 0.2.1, 0.2.3, 0.2.4, 2.3.1, 2.3.2, 2.6.1, 2.7.1, 2.7.2, 4.8.1, 4.8.3, 7.1.1, 7.2.1, 7.4.7, 7.5.1, 7.5.6	3.01.02, 3.03.16	II. 10a

For more details and correlations to other state standards, go to: www.cambridge.org/ventures/correlations

NRS Educational Functioning Level Descriptors	English Language Proficiency and College and Career Readiness Standards
Interpretive ■ Identify the main topic and key details in conversations about major life events in the past. ■ Identify the main topic and key details in a magazine interview. ■ Determine the meaning of common words and phrases related to time lines and events. ■ Determine the main idea and key details on an application for a marriage license. **Productive** ■ Compose a short narrative paragraph about important life events. ■ Use *when* questions and *simple past*, *time phrases*, *someone*, *some*, *anyone*, *everyone*, and *no one*. ■ Use a *comma* after a *time phrase* at the beginning of a sentence. ■ Deliver a short oral presentation on findings from an interview about important life events. **Interactive** ■ Participate in conversations about timelines and major events. ■ Gather and record information from an interview about important life events.	ELP Standards 1–10 Reading Anchors 1, 2, 4, 5, 7, 9, 10 Speaking & Listening Anchors 1, 2, 3, 4, 6
Interpretive ■ Identify the main topic and key details about furniture, appliances, and stores. ■ Identify the main topic and key details in a newspaper article. ■ Determine the meaning of common words and phrases related to comparison shopping. ■ Determine the main idea and key details on a sales receipt. **Productive** ■ Compose a short descriptive paragraph about a gift. ■ Use *comparatives*, *superlatives*, *one*, *the other*, *some*, and *the others*. ■ Use *because* to answer *why* and to give a reason. ■ Deliver a short oral presentation on a picture you created of a room in your house. **Interactive** ■ Participate in conversations about comparison shopping. ■ Gather and record information from a room in your home.	ELP Standards 1–10 Reading Anchors 1, 2, 4, 5, 7, 9, 10 Speaking & Listening Anchors 1, 2, 3, 4, 6
Interpretive ■ Identify the main topic and key details in conversations about completed actions. ■ Identify the main topic and key details in a letter of recommendation. ■ Determine the meaning of common words and phrases related to work history and job skills. ■ Determine the main idea and key details on a timesheet. **Productive** ■ Compose a short summary paragraph about employment history. ■ Use *what are/where* questions, *simple past*, *conjunctions* (and, or but), and *past* and *present* with *could*, *couldn't*, *can*, and *can't*. ■ Deliver a short oral presentation on findings from the Internet about a job application. **Interactive** ■ Participate in conversations about work history and job skills. ■ Gather and record information from the Internet about a job application.	ELP Standards 1–10 Reading Anchors 1, 2, 4, 5, 7, 9, 10 Speaking & Listening Anchors 1, 2, 3, 4, 6
Interpretive ■ Identify the main topic and key details in conversations about recommendations, choices, and polite requests. ■ Identify the main topic and key details in a notice on a notice board. ■ Determine the meaning of common words and phrases related to solving common problems. ■ Determine the main idea and key details on a customer invoice for service and repairs. **Productive** ■ Compose a letter of complaint. ■ Use requests with *can*, *could*, *will*, *would*, *which* questions with *simple present*, and *let's*. ■ Deliver a short oral presentation on findings from interviews about home repairs. **Interactive** ■ Participate in conversations about solving common problems. ■ Gather and record information from interviews about home repairs.	ELP Standards 1-10 Reading Anchors 1, 2, 4, 5, 7, 9, 10 Speaking & Listening Anchors 1, 2, 3, 4, 6
Interpretive ■ Identify the main topic and key details in conversations about making polite offers and responding to offers politely. ■ Identify the main topic and key details in a first-person narrative paragraph about a party. ■ Determine the meaning of common words and phrases related to special occasions. ■ Determine the main idea and key details on a formal invitation to a party. **Productive** ■ Compose a thank-you note for a gift. ■ Use *would you like...*, *direct* and *indirect objects*, *there is/there are*, and *there was/there were*. ■ Deliver a short oral presentation about holidays and celebrations. **Interactive** ■ Participate in conversations about special occasions. ■ Gather and record information from the Internet about holidays and celebrations.	ELP Standards 1-10 Reading Anchors 1, 2, 4, 5, 7, 9, 10 Speaking & Listening Anchors 1, 2, 3, 4, 6

MEET THE **VENTURES** AUTHOR TEAM

(Top row) Dennis Johnson, K. Lynn Savage; (bottom row) Gretchen Bitterlin, Donna Price, and Sylvia G. Ramirez. Together, the *Ventures* author team has more than 200 years teaching ESL as well as other roles that support adult immigrants and refugees, from teacher's aide to dean.

Gretchen Bitterlin has taught Citizenship, ESL, and family literacy through the San Diego Community College District and served as coordinator of the non-credit Continuing Education ESL program. She was an item writer for CASAS tests and chaired the task force that developed the TESOL Adult Education Program Standards. She is recipient of The President's Distinguished Leadership Award from her district and co-author of *English for Adult Competency*. Gretchen holds an MA in TESOL from the University of Arizona.

Dennis Johnson had his first language-teaching experience as a Peace Corps volunteer in South Korea. Following that teaching experience, he became an in-country ESL trainer. After returning to the United States, he began teaching credit and non-credit ESL at City College of San Francisco. As ESL site coordinator, he has provided guidance to faculty in selecting textbooks. He is the author of *Get Up and Go* and co-author of *The Immigrant Experience*. Dennis is the demonstration teacher on the *Ventures Professional Development DVD*. Dennis holds an MA in music from Stanford University.

Donna Price began her ESL career teaching EFL in Madagascar. She is currently associate professor of ESL and vocational ESL / technology resource instructor for the Continuing Education Program, San Diego Community College District. She has served as an author and a trainer for CALPRO, the California Adult Literacy Professional Development Project, co-authoring training modules on contextualizing and integrating workforce skills into the ESL classroom. She is a recipient of the TESOL Newbury House Award for Excellence in Teaching, and she is author of *Skills for Success*. Donna holds an MA in linguistics from San Diego State University.

Sylvia G. Ramirez is a Professor Emeritus at MiraCosta College, a teacher educator, writer, consultant, and a recipient of the California Hayward award for excellence in education, honoring her teaching and professional activities. She is an online instructor for the TESOL Core Certificate. Her MA is in education / counseling from Point Loma University, and she has certificates in ESOL and in online teaching.

K. Lynn Savage first taught English in Japan. She began teaching ESL at City College of San Francisco in 1974, where she has taught all levels of non-credit ESL and has served as Vocational ESL Resource Teacher. She has trained teachers for adult education programs around the country as well as abroad. She chaired the committee that developed *ESL Model Standards for Adult Education Programs* (California, 1992) and is the author, co-author, and editor of many ESL materials including *Crossroads Café*, *Teacher Training through Video*, *Parenting for Academic Success*, *Building Life Skills*, *Picture Stories*, *May I Help You?*, and *English That Works*. Lynn holds an MA in TESOL from Teachers College, Columbia University.

TO THE STUDENT

Welcome to ***Ventures***! The dictionary says that "venture" means a risky or daring journey. Its meaning is similar to the word "adventure." Learning English is certainly a journey and an adventure. We hope that this book helps you in your journey of learning English to fulfill your goals. We believe that this book will prepare you for academic and career courses and give you the English skills you need to get a job or promotion, go to college, or communicate better in your community. The audio, grammar presentations, workbooks, and free Internet practice on the Arcade will help you improve your English outside class. Setting your personal goals will also help. Take a few minutes and write your goals below.

Good luck in your studies!

The Author Team
Gretchen Bitterlin
Dennis Johnson
Donna Price
Sylvia Ramirez
K. Lynn Savage

My goals for studying English

1. My first goal for studying English:	Date: ______
2. My second goal for studying English:	Date: ______
3. My third goal for studying English:	Date: ______

WELCOME

1 Meet your classmates

A Look at the picture. What do you see?

B What are the people doing?

2 Skills

A **Listen.** Amanda is in class. A classmate is interviewing her about her skills. Check (✓) the things Amanda can do.

CD1, Track 2

✓ use a computer	____ read to children	____ write in English
____ speak English	____ speak Spanish	____ speak Russian

Listen again. Check your answers.

B **Read** the list. Check (✓) the things you can do. Add two more skills.

Things I can do in English	
☐ introduce myself	☐ help my child with homework
☐ say my address and telephone number	☐ read to my child
☐ register for a class	☐ read a class schedule
☐ make an appointment with a doctor	☐ read a television schedule
☐ give directions	☐ talk about my weekend
☐ write a shopping list	________________
☐ ask about prices	________________

Talk with a partner. Share your information.

C **Talk** with your classmates. Find classmates with these skills. Complete the chart.

Armin, can you swim?

Yes, I can.

Ask: Can you . . .	Classmate's name
swim?	*Armin*
iron a shirt?	
cook?	
drive a truck?	
paint a house?	
speak three languages?	

USEFUL LANGUAGE
How do you spell that?

Talk with your class. Ask and answer questions.

Who can swim?

Armin can.

Ali can, too.

3 Verb tense review (present and past of *be*)

A **Listen** to each sentence. Check (✓) the correct column.

CD1, Track 3

	am	is	are	was	were
1.	✓				
2.					
3.					
4.					
5.					
6.					
7.					

Listen again. Check your answers.

B **Read** about Maria. Complete the story. Use *am*, *is*, *are*, *was*, *were*, and *weren't*.

My name ___*is*___ (1.) Maria. I _________ (2.) from Mexico. My husband's name _________ (3.) Sergio. He _________ (4.) from Mexico, too. There _________ (5.) three children in our family – one son and two daughters. Our son, Javier, _________ (6.) seven years old. He _________ (7.) born in Mexico. Our daughters, Melisa and Maritza, _________ (8.) twins. They _________ (9.) one year old. They _________ (10.) born in the United States. Sergio and I _________ (11.) born in the United States. We _________ (12.) born in Mexico.

Listen and check your answers.

CD 1, Track 4

C **Talk** with a partner. Ask and answer the questions. Take turns.

1. Where are you from?
2. Were you born there?
3. What was your occupation there?
4. Are you married?
5. How many people are in your family?
6. Is your family here with you?

Share your information with the class.

4 Verb tense review (present and past of regular and irregular verbs)

A **Listen** to each sentence. For each, circle the verb you hear.

CD 1, Track 5

Regular and irregular verbs			
Present	**Past**	**Present**	**Past**
1. (takes)	took	6. takes	took
2. work	worked	7. doesn't buy	didn't buy
3. visits	visited	8. wants	wanted
4. celebrate	celebrated	9. sleeps	slept
5. goes	went	10. don't walk	didn't walk

Listen again. Check your answers.

B **Read** the conversation. Fill in the missing words. Use the correct verb form.

A When did you ______________ (1. come) to this country?

B I ______________ (2. come) here two years ago.

A You speak very well. Did you ______________ (3. study) English here last year?

B Yes, I ______________ (4. do).

A Did you ______________ (5. speak) English in your native country?

B No, I ______________ (6. do).

A What do you usually ______________ (7. do) on the weekend?

B I usually ______________ (8. stay) home, but sometimes I ______________ (9. go) shopping.

Listen and check your answers.

CD 1, Track 6

C **Talk** with your classmates. Ask and answer the questions. Take turns.

1. What do you usually do on the weekend?
2. What did you do last weekend?
3. When did you come to this country?

Share your information with the class.

UNIT 1 PERSONAL INFORMATION

Lesson A Listening

1 Before you listen

A Look at the picture. What do you see?

B Point to: ■ long brown hair ■ straight hair ■ a jogging suit ■ curly blond hair ■ short hair ■ a red shirt ■ a striped skirt

C Describe the people. What are they doing?

2 Listen

A **Listen.** Who is Shoko talking about? Write the letter of the conversation.

CD 1, Track 7

1. ____

2. _a_

3. ____

B **Listen again.** Write *T* (true) or *F* (false).

CD 1, Track 7

Conversation A

1. Victoria is Shoko's daughter. _T_
2. Victoria plays soccer every day. ____
3. Victoria looks like her mother. ____

Conversation B

4. Eddie is Shoko's brother. ____
5. Eddie has a lot of friends. ____
6. Eddie is a very quiet boy. ____

Conversation C

7. Mark is Shoko's husband. ____
8. Mark is a short man. ____
9. Mark studies Spanish. ____

Listen again. Check your answers.

3 After you listen

Talk with a partner. Describe someone in your family.

My mother has long blond hair.

My mother has curly brown hair.

Lesson B She's wearing a short plaid skirt.

1 Grammar focus: adjective order

When you use two or more adjectives, the word order is: 1) size, 2) color, 3) pattern.

QUESTIONS	ANSWERS	
What's she wearing?	She's wearing	**a short plaid** skirt. **a long black and white** coat.

Watch

ADJECTIVE ORDER

Size	Color		Pattern
small	black	purple	
large	blue	red	
short	brown	yellow	
long	green	white	

Pattern

checked

plaid

striped

2 Practice

A **Write.** Complete the conversations. Write the words in the correct order.

1. **A** What's Amy wearing?

   B She's wearing a ___long___ ___black___ dress.
   (black / long)

2. **A** What's she wearing?

   B She's wearing ________ ________ pants.
   (black and white / checked)

3. **A** What does he take to school?

   B He takes a ________ ________ backpack.
   (large / red)

4. **A** What do you usually wear to work?

   B I wear a ________ ________ uniform.
   (blue and white / striped)

5. **A** What's he wearing today?

   B He's wearing a ________ ________ sweater.
   (plaid / red and yellow)

6. **A** What are they wearing?

   B They're wearing ________ ________ skirts.
   (green / short)

7. **A.** What do you like to wear at home?

   B. I like to wear my ________ ________ ________ bathrobe.
   (brown / long / plaid)

8. **A.** What does she wear to the park?

   B. She wears a ________ ________ jogging suit.
   (striped / green and white)

Listen and repeat. Then practice with a partner.

CD 1, Track 8

B **Write** the letter. What are the people wearing?

a. blue plaid pants
b. a long purple coat
c. red shoes
d. a blue checked skirt
e. a short striped dress
f. long black boots
g. a long yellow shirt
h. red and white striped socks
i. a brown sweater
j. a green plaid suit

Talk with a partner. Change the bold words and make conversations.

A What's **Lisa** wearing?
B **She's** wearing a **long yellow shirt**.

USEFUL LANGUAGE
Some clothing items are always plural: *jeans*, *pants*, and *shorts*.

3 Communicate

Talk with a partner about your classmates.

What's Maya wearing?

She's wearing jeans and a long green sweater.

Lesson C What are you doing right now?

1 Grammar focus: present continuous and simple present

Use present continuous for actions happening now. Use simple present for actions happening regularly.

PRESENT CONTINUOUS QUESTIONS			ANSWERS	
What are **you** What**'s** he What **are** they	**doing**	right now? today?	I**'m** He**'s** They**'re**	**watching** TV.

Time words
now
right now
today

Watch

SIMPLE PRESENT QUESTIONS			ANSWERS			
What	**do** you **do** **does** she **do** **do** they **do**	every Tuesday? every day?	I She They	always usually	**go** **goes** **go**	to the park.

Time words
always
usually
every day

2 Practice

A **Write.** Complete the conversations. Use the correct form of the verb.

1. A What *does* Ed *do* (do) every night?
   B He *relaxes* (relax).
   A What ______ Ed ______ (do) right now?
   B He ______ (watch) TV.
2. A What ______ Mary ______ (do) right now?
   B She ______ (teach).
   A What ______ Mary ______ (do) every Tuesday?
   B She ______ (teach).
3. A What ______ Isaac ______ (do) right now?
   B He ______ (study).
   A What ______ Isaac ______ (do) every day?
   B He ______ (go) to class.

Listen and repeat. Then practice with a partner.

CD 1, Track 9

B **Talk** with a partner. Change the **bold** words and make conversations.

A Look! **Betty is leaving early!**
B Of course. **She leaves early** every night.

1. Betty / leave early
2. Antonio / wear jeans and a tie
3. Jin-ho / study alone
4. Olga and Yuri / speak English
5. Yan and Laela / drink coffee
6. Henry / call his wife
7. Antonio / check his phone
8. Olga / wear sunglasses

3 Communicate

A **Talk** with a partner. Ask and answer questions about your routines.

A What do you do on the weekend?
B I usually do things with my children.

A What do you do every night?
B I always study English.

B **Talk** in a group. Ask and answer questions about your classmates right now.

A What's Sara doing right now?
B She's talking to Samuel and Kwan.

Lesson D Reading

1 Before you read

Look at the picture. Answer the questions.

1. Who is the girl?
2. What is she wearing?
3. What is she doing?

2 Read

Read Shoko's email. Listen and read again.

CD 1, Track 10

New Message

Send

Hi Karin,

How are you doing? Guess what! Today is my daughter's birthday. The last time you saw Victoria, she was three years old. Now she's 17! She's tall and very athletic. She likes sports. She plays soccer every afternoon. Here is her photo. She's wearing her red and white striped soccer uniform. She usually wears jeans and a T-shirt. Victoria is also a very good student. She has lots of friends and goes with them to the mall every weekend. How are your daughters? Please send a photo!

Let's stay in touch.

Shoko

Look for a key word or words in the question, and read quickly to find the answer.
How *old* is Victoria?

3 After you read

A Write. Answer the questions about the email. Write complete sentences.

1. What is Shoko's email about? ______
2. What sport does Victoria play? ______
3. What kind of student is Victoria? ______
4. What helps you to understand the word *athletic*? ______
5. How does Shoko feel about Victoria? ______

B Write. Complete the sentences about Victoria.

1. Victoria is very *athletic*______.
2. She likes ______.
3. She has lots of ______.
4. She's wearing ______.

4 Picture dictionary Accessories

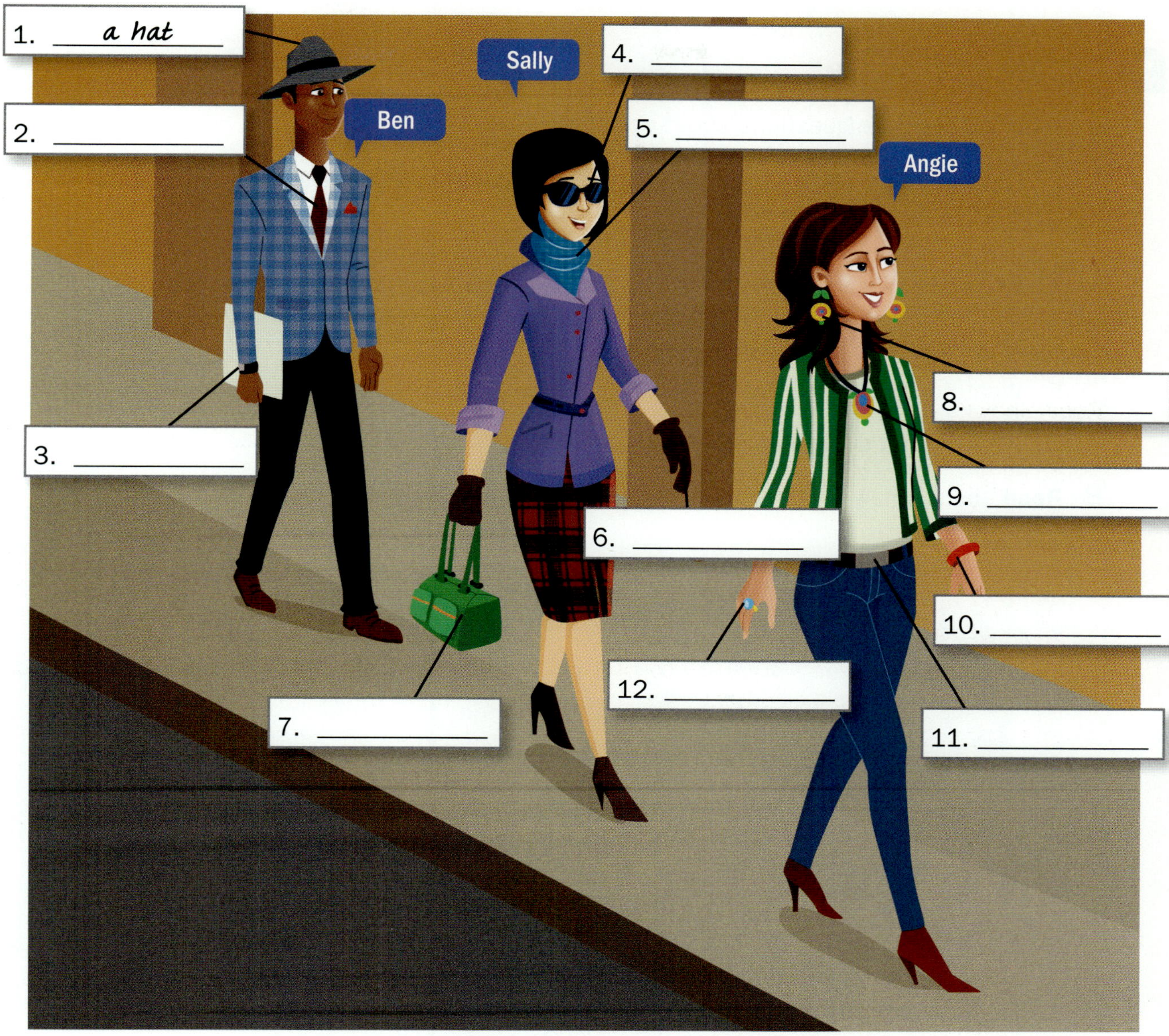

A **Write** the words in the Picture dictionary. Then listen and repeat.

a belt	a hat	a purse	a scarf	a watch	gloves
a bracelet	a necklace	a ring	a tie	earrings	sunglasses

CD 1, Track 11

B **Talk** with a partner. Change the **bold** words and make conversations.

A What's Ben wearing?
B He's wearing **a blue checked jacket.**

A What's Angie wearing?
B She's wearing **large yellow and green earrings.**

For college and career readiness practice, see pages 136–137.

Identify main idea and key details of an email describing someone; use vocabulary for personal accessories

Lesson E Writing

1 Before you write

A **Write.** Answer the questions about yourself.

1. What's your name? ______________________
2. What color is your hair? ______________________
3. What color are your eyes? ______________________
4. What are you wearing? ______________________
5. What do you do after class? ______________________
6. What do you do on the weekend? ______________________

B **Read** about a new classmate.

Introducing: Ricardo Roldan

Ricardo is a new student in our English class. He has short gray hair and brown eyes. Today he is wearing blue plaid pants, a purple sweater, and black shoes. He is also wearing a watch. He is very friendly. After class, Ricardo goes to work. On the weekend, Ricardo helps his wife and fixes things around the house. He also relaxes on the weekend.

C **Write.** Answer the questions about Ricardo. Write complete sentences.

1. Does Ricardo have gray hair or brown hair?
   He has gray hair.
2. Is his hair long or short?
   ____
3. What is he wearing?
   ____
4. What does he do on the weekend?
   ____

D **Write** each sentence in a different way.

1. After class, Ricardo goes to work.
   Ricardo goes to work after class.
2. Tanya goes shopping on the weekend.
   ____
3. Victoria plays soccer every Tuesday.
   ____
4. After work, Henry watches TV.
   ____
5. On the weekend, Yan studies English.
   ____

Time phrases like *after class* or *on the weekend* can come at the beginning or end of a sentence. Use a comma if they are at the beginning.

E **Talk** with a partner. Complete the chart. Use the questions in Exercise 1A.

Partner's name:	
Hair color:	
Eye color:	
Clothing:	
Accessories:	
After-class activities:	
Weekend activities:	

2 Write

Write a paragraph about your partner. Use Exercises 1B and 1E to help you.

3 After you write

A **Read** your paragraph to your partner.

B **Check** your partner's paragraph.

- What did your partner write about you?
- Is the information correct?
- Are the time phrases correct?

Lesson F Another view

1 Life-skills reading

www.webaddress.com

ORDER FORM

ITEM NUMBER	QUANTITY	SIZE	COLOR	ITEM NAME	PRICE
105B	1	L	RED	SWEATER	$29.00
265A	1	M	PURPLE	COAT	$69.00
350G	2	XXL	WHITE	T-SHIRT	$18.00
670F	1	8	BLACK	SHOES	$59.00

METHOD OF PAYMENT

- ☐ Zip Card
- ☑ Master Charge
- ☐ Vista
- ☐ Discovery
- ☐ Debit Card

CREDIT CARD ACCOUNT NUMBER:
8079-1234-3781-4321

EXPIRATION DATE:
12/2020

CUSTOMER NAME:
Bob Nguyen

SUBTOTAL	$175.00
SHIPPING AND HANDLING	$15.00
Under $50..........$5.00	
$50-$100.......... $10.00	
Over $100......... $15.00	
EXPRESS DELIVERY (ADD $5.00)	
TOTAL	$190.00

Cool Clothes
3100 7th St., Portland, Maine 04103, 207-555-4600

USEFUL LANGUAGE

S	small
M	medium
L	large
XL	extra large
XXL	extra extra large

A **Read** the questions. Look at the order form. Fill in the answer.

1. How much is the large red sweater?
   - (A) $18.00
   - (●) $29.00
   - (C) $59.00
   - (D) $69.00

2. In the order form, what word means the same as *fast*?
   - (A) discovery
   - (B) shipping
   - (C) express
   - (D) delivery

3. What color are the T-shirts?
   - (A) black
   - (B) purple
   - (C) red
   - (D) white

4. Which statement is true?
   - (A) The customer is ordering clothing and shoes.
   - (B) The shoes are size 8.
   - (C) The shipping and handling is $15.
   - (D) all of the above

B **Solve** the problem. Which solution is best? Circle your opinion.

Bao ordered and paid for one large red sweater from Clothing Unlimited. After two weeks, he got a package with two large red sweaters. What should he do?

1. Send one sweater back.
2. Keep the two sweaters.
3. Call the company.
4. Other: ______________________________

2 Grammar connections: *and … too, and … either, and but*

Use *and … too*, *and … either*, and *but* to show agreement or difference.

AND … TOO	
Use *and … too* to show agreement with affirmative sentences.	David likes sports, **and** Kyle likes sports, **too**. David likes sports, **and** Kyle does, **too**.
AND … EITHER	
Use *and … either* to show agreement with negative sentences.	David doesn't wear glasses, **and** Kyle doesn't wear glasses **either**. David doesn't wear glasses, **and** Kyle doesn't **either**.
BUT	
Use *but* to show a difference.	Elsa wears glasses, **but** David doesn't wear glasses. Elsa wears glasses, **but** David doesn't.

Watch

A **Work in a group.** Ask questions and complete the chart.

A Do you wear glasses, David?
B No, I don't.

A Do you wear glasses, Kyle?
C No, I don't.

	_______ (name)	_______ (name)	_______ (name)
1. Do you wear glasses?			
2. Do you like sports?			
3. Do you have a job?			
4. Do you usually eat breakfast?			
5. Do you watch TV every night?			
6. Do you usually wear a scarf?			
7. Do you usually wear a hat?			
8. Do you usually wear a watch?			

B **Work with another group.** Talk about two people from your group.

David doesn't wear glasses, *and* Kyle doesn't *either*. David likes sports, *and* Kyle does, *too*.

UNIT 2 AT SCHOOL

Lesson A Listening

1 Before you listen

A Look at the picture. What do you see?

B Point to: ■ an English teacher ■ a computer lab ■ a hall ■ a monitor ■ a lab instructor ■ an ESL classroom ■ a keyboard ■ a mouse

C Look at the people. What are they doing?

2 Listen

A **Listen.** Who is Joseph talking to? Write the letter of the conversation.

CD 1, Track 12

1. ____

2. ____

3. ____

B **Listen again.** Write *T* (true) or *F* (false).

CD 1, Track 12

Conversation A

1. Eva and Joseph are in the computer lab. F
2. Mrs. Lee helped Eva. ____
3. Joseph is taking a keyboarding class. ____

Conversation B

4. Joseph needs to use a computer at work. ____
5. The computer lab is next door to Joseph's classroom. ____
6. Mr. Stephens is the lab instructor. ____

Conversation C

7. Joseph needs to register for a keyboarding class. ____
8. Mrs. Smith works in the computer lab. ____
9. Joseph needs to register next month. ____

Listen again. Check your answers.

3 After you listen

Talk with a partner. Ask and answer the questions.

1. What are some important skills?
2. What new skills do you want to learn?

Lesson B What do you want to do?

1 Grammar focus: *want* and *need* + *to* + verb

Use *want* + *to* + base verb for something you would like to do.
Use *need* + *to* + base verb for something you have to do.

QUESTIONS				ANSWERS		
What	**do**	you	**want** to do?	I	**want**	to learn English.
	does	he		He	**wants**	
	do	they		They	**want**	

QUESTIONS				ANSWERS		
What	**do**	you	**need** to do?	I	**need**	to take an English class.
	does	she		She	**needs**	
	do	they		They	**need**	

Watch

2 Practice

CULTURE NOTE
The GED (General Equivalency Diploma) is a certificate. It is equal to a high school diploma.

A Write. Complete the conversations.

1. **A** What ___*do*___ (do / does) you want to do now?
   B I ___*want to get*___ (want / get) my GED.
2. **A** What ________ (do / does) you need to do?
   B I ________ (need / take) a GED class.
3. **A** What ________ (do / does) Sandra want to do this year?
   B She ________ (want / learn) about computers.
4. **A** What ________ (do / does) the students need to buy?
   B They ________ (need / buy) a student ID card.
5. **A** What ________ (do / does) Ali want to do this year?
   B He ________ (want / make) more money.
6. **A** What ________ (do / does) Celia need to do tonight?
   B She ________ (need / do) her homework.
7. **A** What ________ (do / does) Sergio and Elena want to do next year?
   B They ________ (want / become) citizens.
8. **A** What ________ (do / does) Maria need to do?
   B She ________ (need / make) dinner.

Listen and repeat. Then practice with a partner.

CD 1, Track 13

B **Talk** with a partner. Change the **bold** words and make conversations.

A She wants to **fix cars**. What does she need to do?
B She needs to **study auto mechanics**.
A That's a good idea.

1. she / fix cars study auto mechanics

2. they / learn computer skills take a computer class

3. he / make more money get a second job

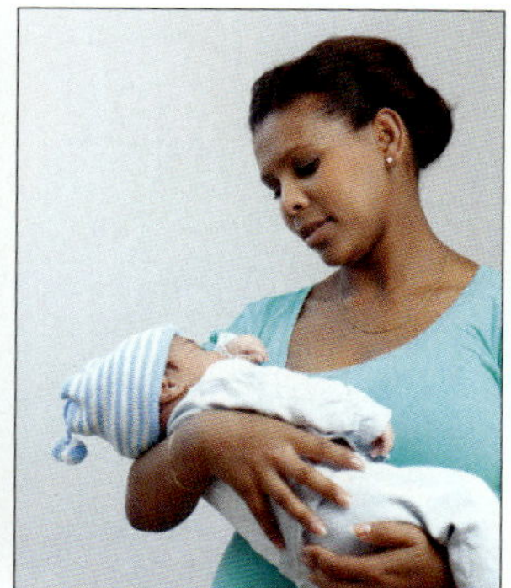

4. she / get a job find a babysitter

5. he / get a driver's license take driving lessons

6. they / become citizens take a citizenship class

7. she / go to college talk to a counselor

8. they / buy a home save more money

3 Communicate

Talk with your classmates. Ask about their goals. Give advice.

What do you want to do?

I want to get a good job.

Why don't you take a computer class?

USEFUL LANGUAGE
Why don't you take a computer class?
You could take a computer class.

Lesson C What will you do?

1 Grammar focus: future with *will*

Use *will / won't* + base form of verb to talk about future definite events or plans.
Add *probably* or *most likely* to show the future events or plans are less certain.

QUESTIONS			ANSWERS		NEGATIVE STATEMENTS		
What **will**	you	**do** next?	I'**ll**	probably **take** conversation classes.	I	probably **won't**	**go** to the party.
	she		She'**ll**		He		
	he		He'**ll**		They		
	they		They'**ll**				

I'll = I will
She'll = She will
He'll = He will
They'll = They will

won't = will not

Watch

2 Practice

A Write. Complete the sentences about Sue's calendar. Use *will* or *won't*.

	MONDAY 7	TUESDAY 8	WEDNESDAY 9	THURSDAY 9	FRIDAY 10	SATURDAY 11
		Study for English Test				Write English paragraph
1 p.m.	1-3 p.m. English Class	1-6 p.m. Work	1-3 p.m. English Class	1-6 p.m. Work	1-3 p.m. English Class	
2 p.m.						2-3 p.m. Salsa Dance Lesson??
3 p.m.	3-4 p.m. Coffee with Ruth		3-4 p.m. Coffee with Ruth?			
4 p.m.	~~4-5 p.m Gym~~		4-5 p.m. Gym		4-5 p.m. Gym	
5 p.m.						
6 p.m.		~~6 p.m. Emily's party~~		6 p.m. Movie with Jose??	6 p.m. Movie with Jose	6 p.m. Family Birthday Party

1. Sue ___will___ go to her English class on Monday. She ___will___ have coffee with Ruth. She ___won't___ go to the gym.
2. Sue has a test on Wednesday. She ________ probably study Tuesday after work. She ________ go to Emily's party.
3. On Wednesday, she ________ go to her English class, and she will go to the gym. Maybe she ________ have coffee with Ruth.
4. She probably ________ go to the movie with Jose on Thursday. She ________ be too tired after work.
5. Sue ________ go to the gym on Friday, and she ________ most likely go to the movie with Jose.
6. On Saturday, Sue ________ write her English paragraph. She probably ________ go to her Salsa dance lesson. She ________ go to the family birthday party.

Listen and repeat. Check your answers.

CD 1, Track 14

B **Talk** with a partner. Change the **bold** words and make conversations.

A What will you do in the next five years?
B Maybe I'll **open a business**.
A That's great!

USEFUL LANGUAGE
Maybe also shows that future plans are less certain. Put *maybe* before the subject for sentences with *will* and *won't*.

1. open a business

2. take a vocational course

3. start business school

4. become citizens

5. go to college

6. learn a new language

7. buy a house

8. take a vacation

3 Communicate

Talk with your classmates. Ask and answer questions about future plans.

A Ming, what will you do next year?
B I'll probably take a vocational course.
A What will you do after that?
B Maybe I'll get a new job. I want to make more money.

Lesson D Reading

1 Before you read

Look at the picture. Answer the questions.

1. Who is the man?
2. Where is he?

2 Read

Read Joseph's application. Listen and read again.

CD 1, Track 15

www.webaddress.com

APPLICATION

What are your future goals? What steps do you need to take?

I want to open my own electronics store. I need to take three steps to reach my goal. First, I need to learn keyboarding. Second, I need to take business classes. Third, I need to work in an electronics store. I will probably open my store in a couple of years.

First, read quickly to get the main idea. Ask yourself, *What is it about?*

3 After you read

A Write. Answer the questions about Joseph. Write complete sentences.

1. What is the reading about? *The reading is about Joseph's goals.*
2. What is Joseph's goal? ______________________
3. What does he need to do first? ______________________
4. What does he need to do second? ______________________
5. When will he open his business? ______________________
6. What word in the reading means *achieve*? ______________________

B Write. Complete the sentences. Use *want/need* and words in the word box.

business	electronics	goal	learn	steps

1. Joseph *wants* (want / need) to have his own store. That is his *goal* .
2. Joseph ________ (want / need) to have his own ________ store.
3. He ________ (want / need) to take three ________ to reach his goal.
4. He ________ (want / need) to ________ keyboarding and take ________ classes.

4 Picture dictionary Vocational courses

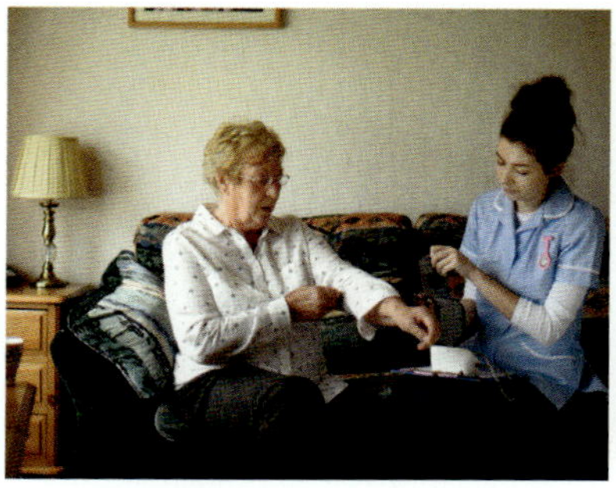

1. home health care

2. ______________

3. ______________

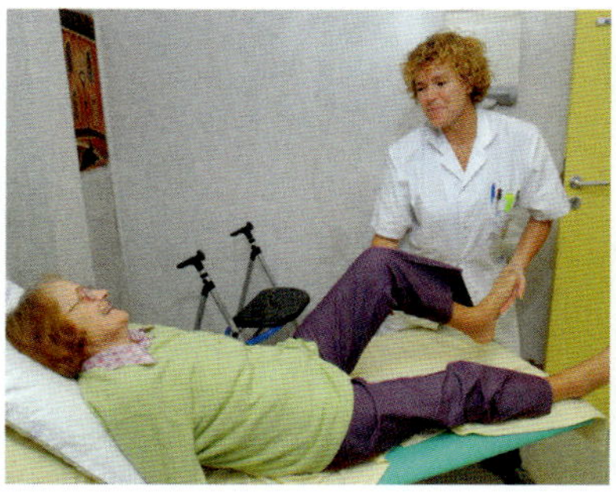

4. ______________

5. ______________

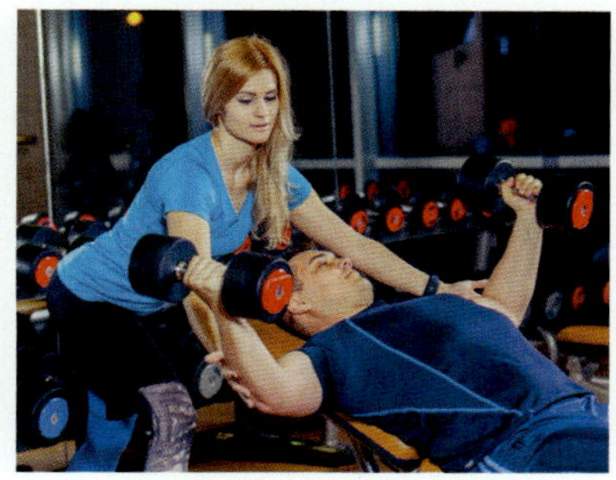

6. ______________

7. ______________

8. ______________

9. ______________

A **Write** the words in the Picture dictionary. Then listen and repeat.

accounting	criminal justice	hotel management
computer networking	fitness training	physical therapy
counseling	home health care	small engine repair

CD 1, Track 16

B **Talk** with a partner. Ask and answer questions.

Do you want to study home health care?

Yes, I do.

Do you want to study counseling?

No, I don't.

For college and career readiness practice, see pages 138–139.

Identify the main idea and key details on an application; use vocabulary for vocational courses

Lesson E Writing

1 Before you write

A **Talk** with a partner. Ask and answer the questions.

1. What are your goals this year?
2. What is your most important goal? Why?
3. What do you need to do to reach your goal?

B **Read** about Angela's goal.

My Goal for Next Year

I have a big goal. I want to help my children with their homework. There are three steps I need to take to reach my goal. First, I need to learn to speak, read, and write English well. Second, I need to volunteer in my children's school. Third, I need to talk with their teachers and learn more about their homework assignments. Maybe I'll be ready to help my children with their homework in a few months.

C **Write.** Complete the chart about Angela's goal.

Angela's goal
She wants to:
help her children with their homework
She needs to:
1. ______________________
2. ______________________
3. ______________________
She will probably reach her goal in:
____

D **Read** Donald's chart. Talk with a partner. Ask and answer the questions.

1. What does Donald want to do?
2. What does he need to do first?
3. What does he need to do second?
4. What does he need to do third?
5. When will he probably reach his goal?

My goal
I want to:
get a job as a security guard
I need to:
1. *take courses in criminal justice*
2. *get a training certificate*
3. *look for jobs in the newspaper and online*
I will probably reach my goal in:
one or two years

E **Write.** Complete the chart about your goal.

My goal
I want to:
____
I need to:
1. ____________________
2. ____________________
3. ____________________
I will probably reach my goal in:
____

2 Write

Write a paragraph about your goal. Write about the steps you need to take. Use Exercises 1B, 1C, 1D, and 1E to help you.

> Begin sentences with words like *First*, *Second*, and *Third* to organize your ideas.

3 After you write

A **Read** your paragraph to a partner.

B **Check** your partner's paragraph.

- What is your partner's goal?
- What are the three steps?
- Did your partner use the words *First*, *Second*, and *Third*?

Lesson F Another view

1 Life-skills reading

www.webaddress.com

COURSE CATALOG

General Equivalency Diploma (GED)

Do you want to get your GED? Then you need to practice your reading, writing, and math skills. Classes are in English or Spanish. No fee.

Instructor: **Mr. Chen** (English), **Ms. Lopez** (Spanish)

Days/Times: Mon, Wed 5:30 p.m. – 7:30 p.m.

Introduction to Computers

This class is for adults who want to learn about computers and the Internet. You will learn about keyboarding, email, and computer jobs. Fee: $75

Instructor: Mrs. Gates

Days/Times: Mon, Wed 7:00 p.m. – 9:00 p.m.

Home Business

Are you tired of working for someone else? Do you need to make more money? You will learn

- 100 home business ideas
- Home business marketing and networking

Fee: $85

Instructor: Mr. Greene

Days/Times: Mon, Tues 6:00 – 8:00 p.m.

Citizenship

Do you want to be an American citizen? First, you need to learn about American history and civics. This class will prepare you for the U.S. citizenship test. Requirements: Legal resident. No fee.

Instructor: Ms. Cuevas

Days/Times: Thurs 7:00 p.m. – 9:00 p.m.

A **Read** the questions. Look at the course catalog. Fill in the answer.

1. Which class is in English or Spanish?
   - (A) Citizenship
   - (B) GED
   - (C) Introduction to Computers
   - (D) Home Business

2. When is the computer class?
   - (A) Monday and Tuesday
   - (B) Monday and Wednesday
   - (C) Tuesday and Thursday
   - (D) Wednesday and Friday

3. What word in the reading means *money*?
   - (A) networking
   - (B) test
   - (C) fee
   - (D) ideas

4. Which courses meet on Mondays and Wednesdays?
   - (A) all courses
   - (B) GED and Home Business
   - (C) GED and Introduction to Computers
   - (D) no courses

B **Solve** the problem. Which solution is best? Circle your opinion.

Rosie is studying to get her GED. She takes the class Mondays and Wednesdays from 5:30 – 7:30. Her employer said she needs computer skills. There is a free class at the same school on Monday and Wednesdays from 7 – 8 p.m. What should she do?

1. Quit the GED course and take the Introduction to Computers Course.
2. Come ½ hour late to the Introduction to Computers course.
3. Talk to a counselor.
4. Other: ____________________

2 Grammar connections: the future with *be going to*, *will*, and the present continuous

There are three ways to talk about future events.

be going to	Martin **is going to make** dinner after class.
will	He **will make** dinner after class.
the present continuous	He**'s making** dinner after class.

Watch

A **Work in a group.** Ask questions and complete the chart.

A What *are* you *going to do* after class?
B I'*m going* to make dinner.
A What *are* you *doing* tomorrow?
B I'*m going* shopping.

	______ (name)	______ (name)
1. What are you going to do after class?		
2. What are you doing tomorrow?		
3. What time will you get up tomorrow?		
4. What are you going to wear tomorrow?		
5. What are you doing next weekend?		
6. What class will you take next semester?		
7. Where will you go on your next vacation?		

B **Share** your group's information with the class.

Martin is going to make dinner after class.
He's going shopping tomorrow. He . . .

Scan a course catalogue for key details; contrast three ways to talk about the future

REVIEW

1 Listening

CD 1, Track 17

Read the questions. Then listen and circle the answers.

1. How old is Fernando?
   a. 25
   (b.) 35
2. What color is his hair?
   a. brown
   b. black
3. Where does he go in the morning?
   a. to school
   b. to work
4. What does he do at Green's Grocery Store?
   a. He's a cashier.
   b. He's a computer technician.
5. When does Fernando play soccer?
   a. on Saturday
   b. on Sunday
6. What does Fernando want to study?
   a. computer repair
   b. computer technology

Talk with a partner. Ask and answer the questions. Use complete sentences.

2 Grammar

A Write. Complete the story.

AN IMPORTANT DAY

Tan Nguyen __is__ (1. be) 45 years old. He is a home health assistant. He ________ (2. want / be) a nurse. He ________ (3. work) from 8:00 a.m. to 4:00 p.m., but today he ________ (4. not / work). This afternoon, he and his wife ________ (5. become) United States citizens. Every day at work, Tan ________ (6. wear) a uniform. Today he ________ (7. wear) a new blue suit, a white shirt, and a red and white striped tie. Tan is very excited.

B Write. Look at the answers. Write the questions.

1. **A** How old __is Tan__?
   B Tan is 45 years old.
2. **A** What ________?
   B He is a home health assistant.
3. **A** When ________?
   B He usually works from 8:00 a.m. to 4:00 p.m.
4. **A** What ________?
   B Today he is wearing a blue suit, a white shirt, and a striped tie.

Talk with a partner. Ask and answer the questions.

3 Pronunciation: strong syllables

A **Listen** to the syllables in these words.

paper   restaurant   computer

CD 1, Track 18

B **Listen and repeat.** Clap for each syllable. Clap loudly for the strong syllable.

● •	• ●	● • •	• ● •	● • • •
necklace	cashier	medium	mechanic	television
keyboard	career	counselor	tomorrow	citizenship
bracelet	repair	uniform	computer	
sweater	achieve	manager	eraser	
jacket		citizen		

CD 1, Track 19

Talk with a partner. Take turns. Say each word. Your partner claps for each syllable.

C **Listen** for the strong syllable in each word. Put a dot over the strong syllable.

1. instructor
2. partner
3. enroll
4. dictionary
5. business
6. sunglasses
7. management
8. relax
9. important

CD 1, Track 20

D **Write** eight words from Units 1 and 2. Put a dot over the strong syllable in each word.

1.	5.
2.	6.
3.	7.
4.	8.

Talk with a partner. Read the words.

UNIT 3 FRIENDS AND FAMILY

Lesson A Listening

1 Before you listen

A Look at the picture. What do you see?

B Point to: ■ a broken-down car ■ smoke ■ groceries ■ a trunk ■ a worried woman ■ an overheated engine ■ a hood

C Look at the people. What happened?

UNIT GOALS

Describe events in chronological order **Write** a journal entry about past activities
Interpret information about cell phone calling plans

2 Listen

A **Listen.** Who is Rosa talking to? Write the letter of the conversation.

CD 1, Track 21

1. ____

2. ____

3. ____

B **Listen again.** Write *T* (true) or *F* (false).

CD 1, Track 21

Conversation A

1. Rosa calls her boss. __F__
2. Rosa's husband is going to come from work. ____
3. Rosa knows the problem with the car. ____

Conversation B

4. Mike works at a coffee shop. ____
5. Mike will pick up the car this afternoon. ____
6. Mike will pick up Rosa and her children. ____

Conversation C

7. Ling needs a ride to school tonight. ____
8. Rosa usually leaves her house at 7:00. ____
9. Ling will pick up Rosa at 8:00. ____

Listen again. Check your answers.

3 After you listen

Talk with a partner. Ask and answer the questions.

1. Did you ever ask a friend for help? If yes, what happened?
2. Did a friend or family member ever ask you for help? If yes, what happened?

Lesson B What did you do last weekend?

1 Grammar focus: simple past with regular and irregular verbs

Use the simple past for actions completed in the past. Add *-ed* to regular verbs. Irregular verbs have different endings.

QUESTIONS			ANSWERS		
What **did**	you she	**do** last weekend?	I She	**stayed** **went**	home. to a party.

QUESTIONS			ANSWERS						
Did	he they	**stay** home last weekend? **go** to a party last weekend?	Yes,	he they	**did.**	No,	he they	**didn't.**

Watch

Regular verbs

fix	→ fixed	stay	→ stayed
grill	→ grilled	study	→ studied
listen	→ listened	watch	→ watched
play	→ played		

Irregular verbs

buy	→ bought	have	→ had
drive	→ drove	meet	→ met
eat	→ ate	read	→ read
go	→ went	take	→ took

2 Practice

A **Write.** Complete the conversations. Use *did* or *didn't* and the simple past form of the verb.

1. **A** What *did* Dahlia and her friends do on Sunday?
   B They *grilled* (grill) hamburgers.
2. **A** What ______ the children do on Thursday?
   B They ______ (take) a walk in the park.
3. **A** What ______ your family do last weekend?
   B We ______ (drive) to the beach.
4. **A** What ______ Sarah do Monday night?
   B She ______ (go) to the movies.
5. **A** What ______ Nikos do Saturday morning?
   B He ______ (fix) the car.
6. **A** ______ Carlos ______ (buy) groceries yesterday?
   B No, he ______.
7. **A** ______ Ana ______ (study) last night?
   B Yes, she ______.
8. **A** ______ Pedro ______ (meet) his friend at the airport last Saturday?
   B No, he ______.
9. **A** ______ the Lopez family ______ (have) a party at their house last weekend?
   B Yes, they ______.
10. **A** ______ Maria and her husband ______ (play) cards on Friday night?
    B No, they ______.

Listen and repeat. Then practice with a partner.

CD 1, Track 22

B **Talk** with a partner. Change the **bold** words and make conversations.

> **A** What did **Alicia** do last weekend?
> **B** **She went shopping** and **read a book**.

Alicia | John | Lisa and Sam

go shopping

eat in a restaurant

have a picnic

read a book

listen to music

play soccer

C **Talk** with a partner. Change the **bold** words and make conversations. Look at the pictures in Exercise 2B.

> **A** Did **Alicia go shopping** last weekend?
> **B** **Yes, she did.**

> **A** Did John **play soccer** last weekend?
> **B** **No, he didn't. He listened to music.**

1. Alicia / go shopping
2. John / play soccer
3. Sam and Lisa / read a book
4. John / eat in a restaurant
5. Alicia / have a picnic
6. Sam and Lisa / play soccer
7. Alicia / read a book
8. John / have a picnic
9. Sam and Lisa / go shopping
10. John / listen to music

3 Communicate

Talk with your classmates. Ask and answer questions about last weekend.

> **A** Karen, did you go to the beach last weekend?
> **B** No, I didn't. I stayed home.

> **A** Marco, what did you do last weekend?
> **B** I studied for a test.

Lesson C When do you usually play soccer?

1 Grammar focus: simple present vs. simple past

Use the simple present for repeated, usual, or daily actions. Use the simple past for actions completed at a specific time in the past.

SIMPLE PRESENT

When What time	**do** **does** **do**	you he they	usually **play** soccer?	I He They	usually	**play** soccer **plays** soccer **play** soccer	on Sunday. at 10:00.

SIMPLE PAST

When What time	**did**	you she they	**play** soccer yesterday?	I She They	**played** soccer	after lunch. at noon.

Watch

2 Practice

A Write. Complete the conversations. Use the simple present or the simple past.

1. **A** When ______ does ______ Sharon usually meet her friends?
   B She usually ______ meets ______ her friends after work.
   A When ______ did ______ Sharon meet her friends yesterday?
   B Yesterday, she ______ met ______ them at noon for lunch.

2. **A** What time ______________ Roberto and Selma usually eat dinner?
   B They usually ______________ dinner at 7:00.
   A When ______________ they eat dinner last night?
   B They ______________ dinner at 8:00.

3. **A** When ______________ Irma and Ron usually study?
   B They usually ______________ on Saturday.
   A When ______________ they study last weekend?
   B They ______________ on Friday night.

4. **A** When ______________ you usually watch movies?
   B I usually ______________ movies after dinner.
   A What time ______________ you watch a movie last night?
   B I ______________ a movie at 6:00.

Listen and repeat. Then practice with a partner.

CD 1, Track 23

B **Talk** with a partner. Change the **bold** words and make conversations.

> **A** When does Karim usually **go to the gym**?
> **B** He usually **goes to the gym** at **7:00 a.m.**

1.

2.

3.

4.

1. go to the gym / 7:00 a.m.
2. take a shower / 9:00 a.m.
3. eat lunch / 1:00 p.m.
4. go to work / 2:00 p.m.

C **Talk** with a partner. Change the **bold** words and make conversations.

> **A** When did Maria **get up** last Saturday?
> **B** She **got up** at **8:00 a.m.**

1.

2.

3.

4.

5.

6.

7.

8.

1. get up / 8:00 a.m.
2. eat breakfast / 8:30 a.m.
3. go shopping / 10:00 a.m.
4. go to her citizenship class / 1:00 p.m.
5. clean her apartment / 6:00 p.m.
6. go to the movies / 7:30 p.m.
7. get home / 10:00 p.m.
8. go to bed / 11:00 p.m.

3 Communicate

Talk with your classmates. Ask and answer questions about daily activities.

When do you usually get up?

I usually get up at 7:00 a.m.

When did you get up this morning?

I got up at 7:30 a.m.

Lesson D Reading

1 Before you read

Look at the picture.
Answer the questions.

1. Who is the woman?
2. What is she thinking about?

2 Read

Read Rosa's journal. Listen and read again.

CD 1, Track 24

Thursday, June 20th

Today was a bad day! On Thursday, my children and I usually go to the park for a picnic, but today we had a problem. We drove to the store to buy groceries, and then the car broke down. I checked the engine, and there was a lot of smoke. I think the engine overheated. Luckily, I had my cell phone! First, I called my husband at work. He left early, picked us up, and took us home. Next, I called the mechanic. Finally, I called Ling and asked for a ride to school tonight. In the end, we didn't go to the park because it was too late. Instead, we had a picnic in our backyard. Then, Ling drove me to school.

Look for these words: *First, Next, Finally*. They tell the order of events.

3 After you read

A **Write.** Answer the questions about Rosa's day. Write complete sentences.

1. What is the main idea of Rosa's journal for June 20th?
2. Where do Rosa and her children go on Thursday?
3. Why was today a bad day?
4. Who did Rosa call first?
5. What did Ling do?
6. What words in the journal help you understand the word *overheated*?

B **Number** the sentences in the correct order.

_____ Ling drove Rosa to school.

_____ Rosa called her husband at work.

_____ Rosa's husband took them home.

__*1*__ Rosa went to the store.

_____ The car broke down.

4 Picture dictionary Daily activities

1. make lunch

2. ______

3. ______

4. ______

5. ______

6. ______

7. ______

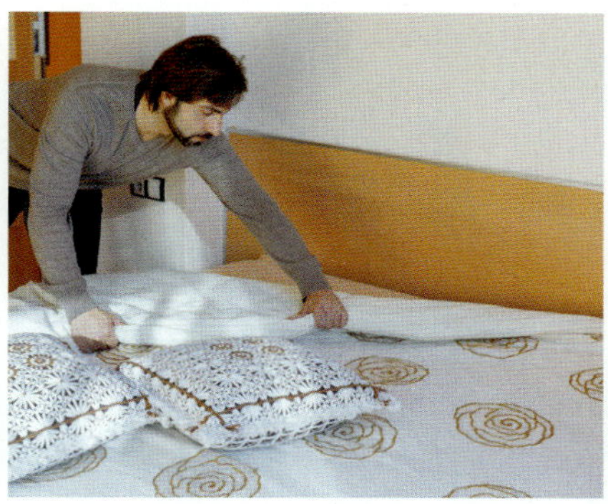

8. ______

9. ______

A **Write** the words in the Picture dictionary. Then listen and repeat.

do homework	do the laundry	get up	make the bed	take a nap
do the dishes	get dressed	make lunch	take a bath	

CD 1, Track 25

B **Talk** with a partner. Change the bold words and make conversations.

A Did you **do the laundry** yesterday?
B Yes, I did.

A Did you **make the bed** this morning?
B No, I didn't. **I got up late**.

For college and career readiness practice, see pages 140–141.

Lesson E Writing

1 Before you write

A **Write.** Think about a day last week. Draw three pictures about that day. Write a sentence about each picture. Use the simple past.

1.

2.

3.

1. ______________________________
2. ______________________________
3. ______________________________

Talk with a partner. Share your pictures and sentences.

B **Read** Tina's journal.

Tuesday, September 1

Last Saturday, I went shopping. I bought five bags of food. I put the groceries in the trunk of my car. Then, I drove home. When I got home, I didn't have my purse. It wasn't in the car, and it wasn't in the trunk. First, I drove back to the store. Next, I looked for my purse outside by the shopping carts, but I didn't find it. Finally, I went inside and asked the manager about my purse. He looked and found my purse in the Lost and Found. I was very happy. In the end, it was a good day.

CULTURE NOTE
Many places have a *Lost and Found*. Go there to find lost things.

C **Write.** Answer the questions about Tina's day. Write complete sentences.

1. When did Tina go shopping? *She went shopping last Saturday.*
2. Where did she put the groceries? ______________________________
3. Where did she first look for her purse? ______________________________
4. Where was her purse? ______________________________

D **Write** Read the sentences. Write ***First***, ***Next***, or ***Finally*** on the correct line.

> Use a comma after sequence words.
> *First, I washed the dirty clothes.*

1. Last Saturday, I did the laundry.

   ____________, I dried the clothes in the dryer.

   ____________, I folded the clean clothes.

   ___*First*___, I washed the dirty clothes.

2. Last night, I stayed home.

   ____________, I washed the dishes.

   ____________, I cooked dinner.

   ____________, I went to bed.

3. Last Thursday, my family had a picnic.

   ____________, we ate breakfast.

   ____________, we woke up early.

   ____________, we went to the park.

E **Write** the sentences from Exercise 1D in the correct order.

1. *Last Saturday, I did the laundry. First, I washed the dirty clothes. Next, ...*

   ____

   ____

2. ____

   ____

   ____

3. ____

   ____

   ____

2 Write

Write a journal entry about a day in your life. Use Exercises 1A, 1B, and 1E to help you.

3 After you write

A **Read** your journal entry to a partner.

B **Check** your partner's journal entry.

- What kind of day did your partner have?
- What happened first?
- Are there commas after the sequence words (*First*, *Next*, *Finally*)?

Lesson F Another view

1 People Have Different Views About Cell Phones

People Have Different Views About When It Is OK Or Not OK To Use Their Cellphones

% of adults who believe it is OK or not to use a cellphone in these situations

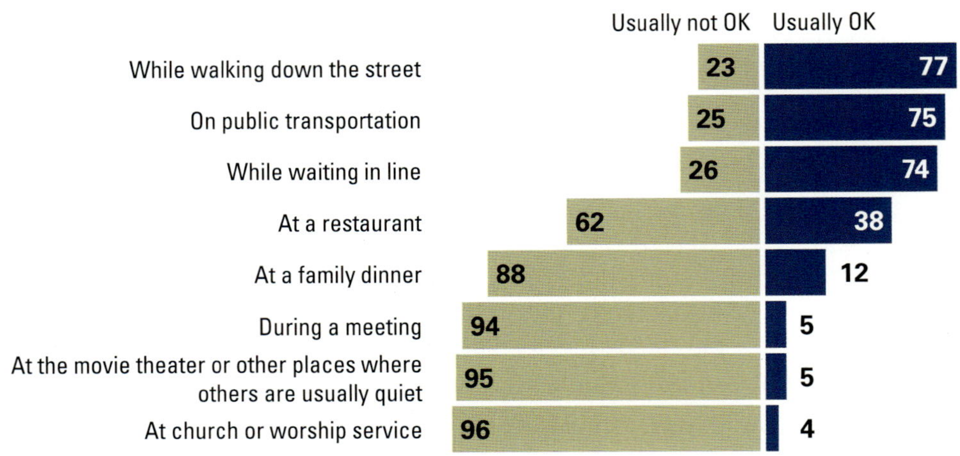

Source: Pew Research Center American Trends Panel survey, May 30–June 30, 2014.

A **Read** the questions. Look at the information about cell phone use. Fill in the answer.

1. According to this study, what percent of adults think it is OK to use a cell phone at a family dinner?
   - (A) 4%
   - (B) 12%
   - (C) 88%
   - (D) 96%

2. According to this study, when is the worst time to use a cell phone?
   - (A) at a restaurant
   - (B) when waiting in line
   - (C) at church
   - (D) during a meeting

3. When do most people think it is OK to use a cell phone?
   - (A) walking down the street
   - (B) waiting in line
   - (C) on public transportation
   - (D) all of the above

4. In the phrase *People have different views*, what does the word *views* mean?
   - (A) opinions
   - (B) problems
   - (C) examples
   - (D) facts

B **Solve** the problem. Which solution is best? Circle your opinion.

Jose is in English class. He cannot find his cell phone. Maybe he left it in the cafeteria before class. What should he do?

1. Leave class now to look for his phone.
2. Wait until the break time to leave class.
3. Ask the teacher to make an announcement about his lost phone.
4. Other: ______________________________

2 Grammar connections: *make* and *do; play* and *go*

Use *make*, *do*, *play* and *go* in different situations.

Use *do* to talk about most chores. Exception: *make the bed*	Did you **do the dishes**? We **did the laundry** after school.
Use *make* for activities when you create or build something.	My mother **made a dress**. I **made lunch**. / I **made tacos**.
Use *play* with many sports, games, and musical instruments.	My brother **plays baseball** well. I **play board games** with my friends. Jenna **plays the guitar**.
Use *go* + verb + *ing* for activities.	I usually **go jogging** in the morning. Do you **go shopping** on the weekends?

Watch

A **Work with a partner.** Write the words under the correct verb.

biking breakfast cards chess chores dancing dinner fishing football hiking homework housework jewelry laundry piano pizza

Do	Make	Play	Go
			biking

B **Work in a group.** Choose a word from 2A. Act out the activity in front of your group. Your classmates guess.

A Are you playing chess?

B No, I'm not.

A Are you playing the piano?

B Yes, I am.

UNIT 4 HEALTH

Lesson A Listening

1 Before you listen

A Look at the picture. What do you see?

B Point to: ■ crutches ■ an injured hand ■ broken bones ■ a sprained ankle ■ an inhaler ■ an X-ray ■ a painful knee

C Where are these people? What happened to them?

2 Listen

A **Listen.** Who is Hamid talking to? Write the letter of the conversation.

CD 1, Track 26

1. ____

2. ____

3. ____

B **Listen again.** Write *T* (true) or *F* (false).

CD 1, Track 26

Conversation A

1. Hamid had an accident at home. F
2. Hamid fell off a ladder. ____
3. Hamid will pick up his children. ____

Conversation B

4. Hamid had to get an X-ray. ____
5. Chris can't drive Hamid home. ____
6. The hospital is on 53rd Street. ____

Conversation C

7. Mr. Jackson will fill out an accident report. ____
8. Hamid has to finish the paint job. ____
9. Hamid will stay home tomorrow. ____

Listen again. Check your answers.

3 After you listen

Talk with a partner. Ask and answer the questions.

1. What jobs are dangerous? Why?
2. Did you ever have an accident at work? What happened?
3. Did you ever have an accident at home? What happened?

Lesson B You should go to the hospital.

1 Grammar focus: *should* and *shouldn't*

Use *should* and *shouldn't* before a base verb to give advice or an opinion.

QUESTIONS				ANSWERS					
What	**should**	I	do?	You	**should**	go to the hospital.	You	**shouldn't**	work.
		we		We			We		
		he		He			He		
		she		She			She		
		they		They			They		

shouldn't = should not

Watch

2 Practice

A Write. Complete the conversations. Use *should* or *shouldn't*.

1. **A** Ken's eyes hurt. What ___should___ he do?
   B He should rest. He ___shouldn't___ read right now.

2. **A** They have stomachaches. What ____________ they do?
   B They ____________ eat. They ____________ take some medicine.

3. **A** My tooth hurts. What ____________ I do?
   B You ____________ see a dentist.

4. **A** Mia has a headache. What ____________ she do?
   B She ____________ take some aspirin.

5. **A** I hurt my leg. What ____________ I do?
   B You ____________ get an X-ray.
   You ____________ walk.

6. **A** I have a bottle of medicine.
   What ____________ I do?
   B You ____________ read the label.
   You shouldn't keep it in a hot place.

7. **A** We are very tired. What should we do?
   B We ____________ rest. We ____________ work so hard.

Listen and repeat. Then practice with a partner.

CD 1, Track 27

B **Look** at the pictures of Alan. He is gardening. It's very hot. Check (✓) the things he should do.

☐ Drink lots of water.

☐ Wear heavy clothes.

☐ Take a break.

☐ Use a wet towel.

☐ Stay in the sun.

☐ Stay in the shade.

Talk with a partner. Look at the pictures again. Change the **bold** words and make conversations.

A Alan doesn't feel well. What should he do?

B He should **drink lots of water**. He shouldn't **stay in the sun**.

A OK. I'll tell him.

USEFUL LANGUAGE

I'll tell him.

I'll let him know.

3 Communicate

Talk in a group. Read the problems. Give advice.

1. Teresa's wrist is very sore. What should she do?

2. Ed is very hot. He doesn't feel well. What should he do?

3. Susana fell off her chair. What should her mother do?

Lesson C You have to see a doctor.

1 Grammar focus: *have to* + verb

Use *have to* before a base verb to indicate something is necessary.

QUESTIONS				ANSWERS		
What	**do**	I	**have** to do?	You	**have to**	see a doctor.
	does	he		He	**has to**	
	does	she		She	**has to**	
	do	they		They	**have to**	

Watch

2 Practice

A **Write.** Complete the conversations. Use *have to* or *has to*.

1. **A** Elian hurt his leg.
   B He ___has to___ get an X-ray.
2. **A** Kathy and Tom have asthma.
   B They ____________ take their medicine.

3. **A** Are your eyes bad?
   B Yes, they are. I ____________ wear glasses.
4. **A** Marcia has a sprained ankle.
   B She ____________ get a pair of crutches.
5. **A** Nick and Tony had an accident at work.
   B They ____________ fill out an accident report.

6. **A** Pam hurt her back.
   B She ____________ go home early.
7. **A** Do you have asthma?
   B Yes, I do. I ____________ use an inhaler.
8. **A** My son broke his arm.
   B You ____________ take him to the hospital.

Listen and repeat. Then practice with a partner.

CD 1, Track 28

B **Talk** with a partner. Change the **bold** words and make conversations.

A Here's your prescription. You have to **keep** this medicine **in the refrigerator**.

B OK. I have to **keep** this medicine **in the refrigerator**.

A Yes. Call me if you have any questions.

CULTURE NOTE
Warning labels on medicine say what you should and shouldn't do.

3 Communicate

Talk with a partner. What happened to these people? What do they have to do?

1.

2.

3.

She burned her hand.

She has to see a doctor.

Lesson D Reading

1 Before you read

Look at the picture. Answer the questions.

1. Who is the man?
2. What is he doing?
3. What should he do?

2 Read

Read the warning label. Listen and read again.

CD 1, Track 29

WARNING: PREVENT ACCIDENTS. READ BEFORE USING!

- Face the ladder when climbing up and down.
- Don't carry a lot of equipment while climbing a ladder – wear a tool belt.
- Never stand on the shelf of the ladder – stand on the steps.
- Never stand on the top step of a ladder.
- Be safe! Always read and follow the safety stickers.

Lists often begin with a number or bullet (•). Each numbered or bulleted item is a new idea.

3 After you read

A **Write.** Answer the questions.

1. What is the purpose of the warning?
2. Why should you wear a tool belt?
3. What is another word for *prevent*?
4. Why shouldn't you stand on the top step of a ladder?
5. Why do we read safety stickers?

B **Write.** Complete the paragraph. Words can be used more than once.

CULTURE NOTE
In emergencies, dial 911 for help.

accidents	ladder	safe	safety	shelf	should	shouldn't	tool belt

Be Careful in the Workplace!

Don't have *accidents* (1) at work. Always read the ________ (2) stickers on your tools and equipment. When you climb a ________ (3), wear a ________ (4). When you carry heavy items, ask someone to help you. You ________ (5) carry a lot of equipment. You ________ (6) stand on the steps. You ________ (7) stand on the ________ (8). When climbing up or down, you ________ (9) face the ladder. We want our workers to be ________ (10) and healthy.

4 Picture dictionary Health problems

1. a swollen knee

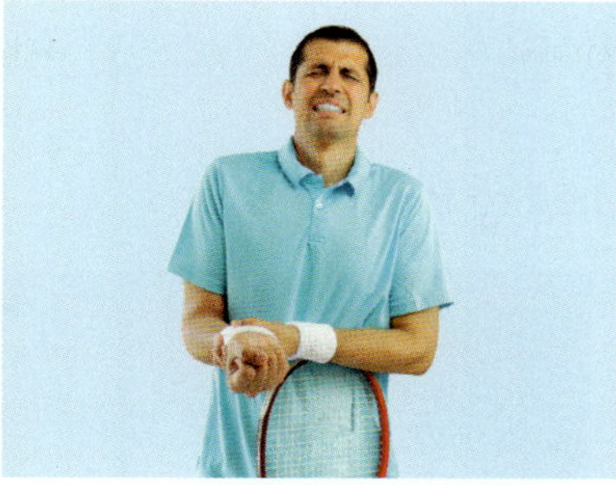

2. ______________

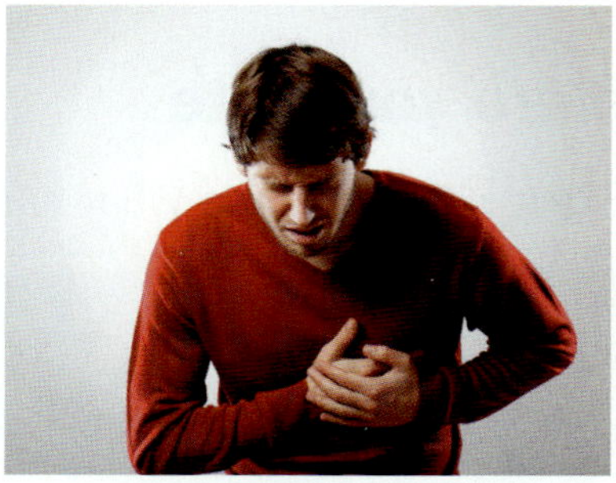

3. ______________

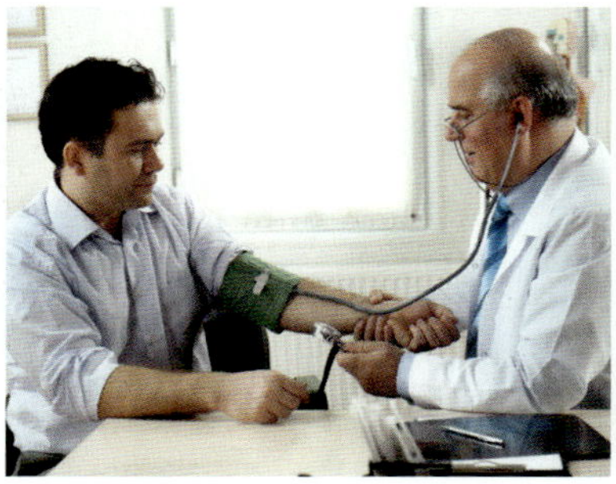

4. ______________

5. ______________

6. ______________

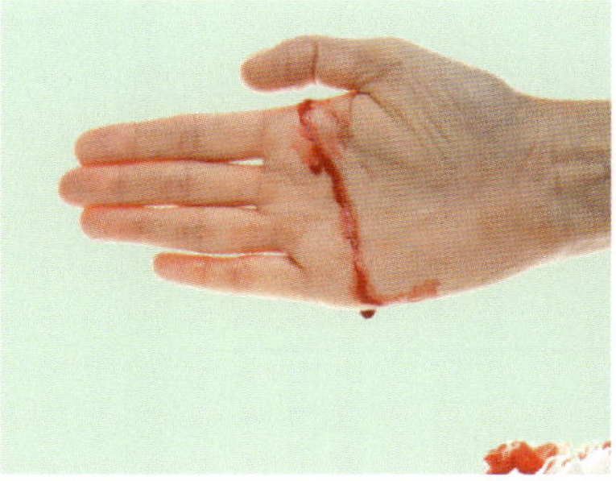

7. ______________

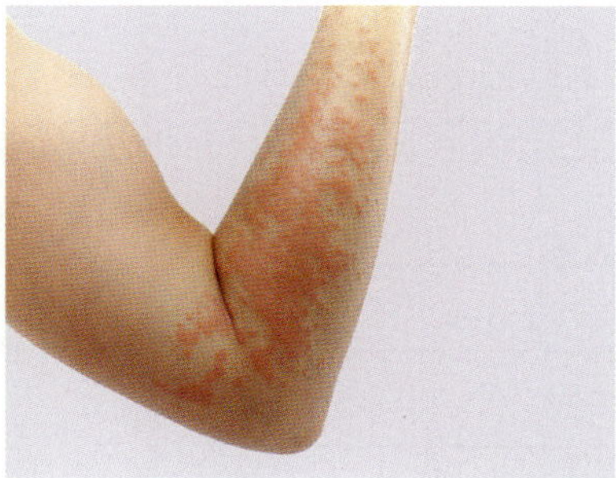

8. ______________

9. ______________

A **Write** the words in the Picture dictionary. Then listen and repeat.

a bad cut	a stiff neck	chest pains
a rash	a swollen knee	chills
a sprained wrist	allergies	high blood pressure

CD 1, Track 30

B **Talk** with a partner. Change the **bold** words and make conversations.

A **She** has **a swollen knee**. What should **she** do?

B **She** should **stay in bed and use ice**.

For college and career readiness practice, see pages 142–143.

Identify the main idea and key details on a warning label; use vocabulary for health problems

Lesson E Writing

1 Before you write

A **Talk** with a partner. What happened to this woman?

B **Read** the accident report.

ACCIDENT REPORT FORM

Employee name: *Komiko Yanaka*

Date of accident: *September 13, 2018* Time: *9:00 p.m.*

Type of injury: *cut foot*

How did the accident happen? *Last night, I was in the kitchen. Every night, I cut vegetables. Last night, the knife fell and cut my foot. I had to go to the doctor.*

Signature: *Komiko Yanaka* Date: *9/14/18*

C **Write.** Answer the questions about the accident report.

1. Who had an accident? *Komiko Yanaka*
2. When did the accident happen? __________
3. What was the injury? __________
4. How did the injury happen? __________
5. When did she sign the form? __________

D **Write.** Work with a partner. Read the sentences. Number the sentences in the correct order.

1. Yesterday, I cut my foot.
   ____ It fell on my foot.
   ____ The knife fell.
   __1__ I was in the kitchen.
2. Yesterday, I sprained my ankle.
   ____ There was water on the floor.
   ____ I have to fill out an accident report.
   ____ I slipped.
3. Yesterday, I broke my leg.
   ____ I fell off the ladder.
   ____ I went to the hospital.
   ____ I was at the top of a ladder.
4. Yesterday, I hurt my back.
   ____ I felt a terrible pain in my back.
   ____ I picked up a heavy box.
   ____ I have to see a doctor tomorrow.

2 Write

Complete the accident report form. Use your imagination or write about a real accident. Use Exercises 1B and 1D to help you.

ACCIDENT REPORT FORM

Employee name: ____________________

Date of accident: ____________________ Time: ______________

Type of injury: ____________________

How did the accident happen? ______________________________

____

____

____

____

Signature: ____________________ Date: ______________

Your signature on a form makes it official. For a signature, use cursive writing. Don't print.

Carl Stanley

~~Carl Stanley~~

3 After you write

A **Read** your form to a partner.

B **Check** your partner's form.

- What was the injury?
- What was the date of the accident?
- Is there a signature on the form?

Lesson F Another view

1 Life-skills reading

Drug facts	
Active ingredient (in each tablet)	**Purpose**
Acetaminophen 325 mg	Pain reliever
Uses Temporary relief of minor aches and pains	
Warnings	
▪ Ask a doctor or pharmacist before use if you are taking a prescription drug.	
▪ Ask a doctor before use if you have liver or kidney disease.	
▪ When using this product, do not take more than directed.	
▪ Can cause drowsiness.	
▪ Keep out of reach of children.	
Directions	
▪ Adults and children 12 years and over: Take 2 tablets every 4 to 6 hours as needed. Do not take more than 8 tablets in 24 hours.	
▪ Children under 12 years of age: Ask a doctor.	

A Read the questions. Look at the medicine label. Fill in the answer.

1. Why should you take this medicine?
   - (A) for drowsiness
   - (B) for aches and pains
   - (C) for kidney disease
   - (D) for liver disease
2. How many tablets should children under 12 take at one time?
   - (A) 2 tablets
   - (B) 4 tablets
   - (C) no tablets
   - (D) none of the above
3. What does *temporary* mean?
   - (A) definite
   - (B) unlimited
   - (C) a short time
   - (D) a long time
4. How many tablets can an adult take in one day?
   - (A) 8 tablets
   - (B) 12 tablets
   - (C) 24 tablets
   - (D) none of the above

B Solve the problem. Which solution is best? Circle your opinion.

John is a butcher. He cut his finger slicing meat. He needs to get it stitched. What should he do?

1. Leave work immediately to go to the doctor.
2. Show his supervisor and ask what he should do.
3. Use a bandage from the first aid kit and go to the doctor after work.
4. Other: ______________________________

2 Grammar connections: *must, must not, have to, not have to*

Use *must, must not, have to* and *not have* before the base form of a verb.

must, have to = required	You **must take** this medicine three times a day. You **have to take** it three times a day.
must not = not allowed	You **must not drive** after you take it.
not have to = not necessary, but OK	You **don't have to take** it with food, but you can.

Watch

A **Work** with a partner. Write *have to / must*, *must not*, or *don't have to*.

- Take with plenty of water.
- Take one pill three times a day with or without food.

1. You *have to / must* take this medication with water. You also *must / have to* take it three times a day. You ______ take it with food.

- Take once a day with food.
- Do not drive after taking medication.
- Refrigerate medication.

2. You ______ take this medication once a day. You ______ drive after taking it. You ______ keep the medication in the refrigerator.

- Take when needed.
- Stay out of the sun.
- Do not give to children.

3. You ______ take this medication every day. You ______ be in the sun after taking it. You ______ give this medication to children.

- Take twice a day.
- Do not take with grapefruit juice.
- You may refrigerate medication.

4. You ______ take this medication twice a day. You ______ drink grapefruit juice when you take it. You ______ keep it in the refrigerator.

B **Work** with your partner. Have a conversation between a pharmacist and a customer. Use the labels in 2A. Take turns.

A Here's your medication. Remember, you have to take it with water.

B OK. Do I need to eat first?

A You don't have to eat first, but you can. You must take it three times a day.

USEFUL LANGUAGE

OK.

I understand.

Yes, I see.

Scan a medicine label for key details; contrast *must* and *must not* with *have to* and *not have to*

REVIEW

1 Listening

Read the questions. Then listen and circle the answers.

CD 1, Track 31

1. What does Trinh do?
   (a.) She's a nurse.
   b. She's a server.
2. Where does she work?
   a. at a hospital
   b. at a restaurant
3. Who became citizens on Friday?
   a. Trinh and her family
   b. Trinh and her husband
4. What did Trinh and her husband do at the beach?
   a. They took pictures.
   b. They took a nap.
5. When did they grill hamburgers?
   a. in the afternoon
   b. in the evening
6. What did they do at home?
   a. They read.
   b. They watched a movie.

Talk with a partner. Ask and answer the questions. Use complete sentences.

2 Grammar

A Write. Complete the story.

AT THE DOCTOR'S OFFICE

Yesterday, Manuel's wife Serena ___*took*___ (1. take) him to Dr. Scott's office. Dr. Scott __________ (2. tell) Manuel that he __________ (3. should / lose) weight. Manuel usually __________ (4. eat) a lot of fried food. He __________ (5. drink) a lot of coffee and soda. Dr. Scott said Manuel __________ (6. should / eat) more fruit and vegetables and drink more water. She said that Manuel __________ (7. should / exercise). Now he __________ (8. have to) walk every day.

B Write. Look at the answers. Write the questions.

1. **A** *Where did Serena take Manuel?*
   B Serena took Manuel to Dr. Scott's office.
2. **A** What __________________?
   B He usually eats fried food.
3. **A** What __________________?
   B He should eat fruit and vegetables.
4. **A** What __________________?
   B He has to exercise.

Talk with a partner. Ask and answer the questions.

3 Pronunciation: important words

A **Listen** to the important words in these sentences.

Tina's **car** broke down.

Oscar has to take his **medicine**.

CD 1, Track 32

B **Listen and repeat.** Clap for each word. Clap loudly for the important word.

1. His **wife** had to do it.
2. Van has a **headache**.
3. I played **soccer** last night.
4. They went to the **library** yesterday.
5. Eliza **works** in the afternoon.
6. **Sam** made breakfast.

CD 1, Track 33

C **Listen** for the important word in each sentence. Underline the important word.

1. Ali cut his arm.
2. He went to the hospital.
3. His sister took him.
4. He saw the doctor.
5. He has to take some medicine.
6. He shouldn't carry heavy items.

CD 1, Track 34

Talk with a partner. Compare your answers.

D **Write** six sentences from Units 3 and 4. Then work with a partner. Underline the important words in your partner's sentences.

1.
2.
3.
4.
5.
6.

Talk with a partner. Read the sentences.

UNIT 5 AROUND TOWN

Lesson A Listening

1 Before you listen

A Look at the picture. What do you see?

B Point to: ■ an information desk ■ arrivals ■ departures ■ a track ■ a ticket booth ■ a suitcase ■ a waiting area

C Where are these people? What are they doing?

2 Listen

CD 1, Track 35

A **Listen.** What is Binh talking about? Write the letter of the conversation.

1. ____

2. ____

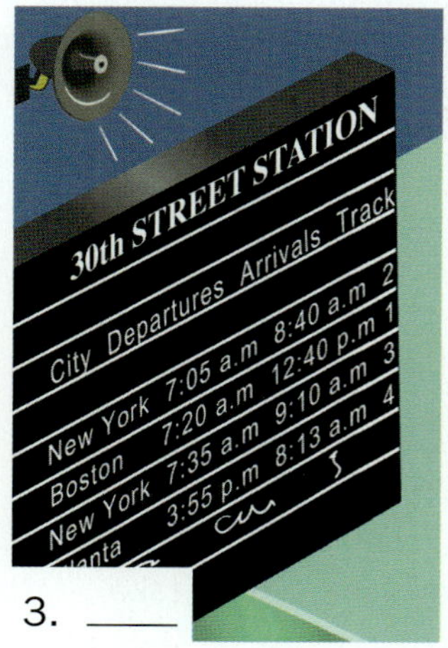

3. ____

B **Listen again.** Write *T* (true) or *F* (false).

CD 1, Track 35

Conversation A

1. Trains to Boston leave every hour. ___T___
2. The next train to Boston will leave at 8:00. ____
3. The next train to Boston will leave from Track 1. ____

Conversation B

4. Trains to New York leave every hour. ____
5. The next train to New York will leave at 7:35. ____
6. Binh and his mother need to buy tickets. ____

Conversation C

7. Binh never travels by train. ____
8. It takes about two hours to drive to New York. ____
9. It takes two and a half hours to get to New York by train. ____

Listen again. Check your answers.

3 After you listen

Talk with a partner. How do you get to work? How do you get to school?

I go to work by bus, and I walk to school.

I take the train to work, and I drive to school.

Lesson B How often? How long?

1 Grammar focus: *How often?* and *How long?*

Use *How often*? to ask about frequency (how many times an event happens). Use *How long*? to ask about duration (how long an event happens).

QUESTIONS				ANSWERS		
How often	do do does	trains you he	go to New York?	They I He	go go goes	every 30 minutes. once a year. twice a month.

Watch

Time phrases for frequency
every 30 minutes — every day — once a week — twice a month — three times a year

QUESTION		ANSWERS	
How long does it take	to go to New York?	It takes	about two hours. around two hours.

Time phrases for duration
about five minutes — a half hour — one hour — an hour and ten minutes — a long time

2 Practice

A **Write.** Circle the correct answers.

1. **A** How often does Binh go to New York?
   B 30 minutes. / (Twice a month.)
2. **A** How long does it take to fly to Mexico?
   B A long time. / Once a month.
3. **A** How often do you study?
   B Three hours. / Twice a week.
4. **A** How long does it take to drive to Toronto?
   B Seven hours. / Once a day.
5. **A** How long does it take to walk to school?
   B Twice a week. / 20 minutes.
6. **A** How often does Sandra cook dinner?
   B Two hours. / Three times a week.
7. **A** How often does the bus go to Springfield?
   B Once a day. / A long time.
8. **A** How often do they go on vacation?
   B A long time. / Once a year.
9. **A** How long does it take to drive to the airport?
   B One hour. / Twice a year.
10. **A** How long does it take to walk to the library?
    B Every 30 minutes. / 25 minutes.

Listen and repeat. Then practice with a partner.

CD 1, Track 36

B **Read** the bus schedule. Where does the bus go?

Springfield to New York City		
Departs	Arrives	Duration
6:30 a.m.	9:00 a.m.	2h 30m
11:00 a.m.	1:30 p.m.	2h 30m
2:00 p.m.	4:30 p.m.	2h 30m
6:30 p.m.	9:00 p.m.	2h 30m

Springfield to Capital Airport		
Departs	Arrives	Duration
5:30 a.m.	6:50 a.m.	1h 20m
9:00 a.m.	10:20 a.m.	1h 20m
3:00 p.m.	4:20 p.m.	1h 20m
5:00 p.m.	6:20 p.m.	1h 20m
6:00 p.m.	7:20 p.m.	1h 20m

Springfield to Boston		
Departs	Arrives	Duration
8:00 a.m.	4:15 p.m.	8h 15m
9:30 a.m.	5:45 p.m.	8h 15m
11:00 a.m.	7:15 p.m.	8h 15m

Springfield to Washington, D.C.		
Departs	Arrives	Duration
7:45 a.m.	11:15 a.m.	3h 30m
9:45 a.m.	1:15 p.m.	3h 30m
11:00 a.m.	2:30 p.m.	3h 30m
1:00 p.m.	4:30 p.m.	3h 30m

h = hour   m = minute

C **Talk** with a partner. Change the **bold** words and make conversations.

A Excuse me. How often do buses go to **New York City**?
B They go **four** times a day.
A How long does it take to get there?
B It takes about **two and a half hours**.

USEFUL LANGUAGE
two and a half hours = two hours and 30 minutes
a half hour = half an hour = 30 minutes
an hour and a half = one hour and 30 minute

1. New York City 2. Boston 3. Washington, D.C. 4. the airport

3 Communicate

Talk with a partner. Ask questions. Complete the chart.

A How often do you walk to school?
B I walk to school every day. **OR** I don't walk to school. I take a bus.

A How long does it take?
B It takes about half an hour.

	How often?	How long?
walk to school	*every day*	*half an hour*
take the bus to work		
drive to the store		
fly to another country		

Use question words *how often, how long*; talk about frequency and duration

Lesson C She often walks to school.

1 Grammar focus: adverbs of frequency

With most verbs, adverbs of frequency go between the subject and verb. With the verb *be*, adverbs of frequency go after the verb.

STATEMENTS

She	**often** **sometimes** **rarely** **never**	walks to school.	She is	**always** **usually** **rarely** **never**	late for class.

Watch

Adverbs of frequency

always	100% frequency
usually / often	↑
sometimes	
hardly ever / rarely	
never	0%

2 Practice

A **Write.** Use adverbs of frequency and make new sentences.

1. Teresa drives to work in the morning.
   Teresa always drives to work in the morning.
   (always)
2. She is late.
   ____
   (rarely)
3. Her husband walks to work.
   ____
   (usually)
4. He takes a taxi.
   ____
   (sometimes)
5. He drives.
   ____
   (never)
6. Their daughter rides her bike to school.
   ____
   (always)
7. She is tired in the morning.
   ____
   (often)
8. Her daughter is absent from school.
   ____
   (rarely)
9. Teresa goes to the library on Sunday.
   ____
   (never)
10. Her husband is sick.
    ____
    (hardly ever)

Listen and repeat. Check your answers.

CD 1, Track 37

B **Talk** with a partner. Change the **bold** words and make conversations.

John	Never	Hardly ever	Usually	Always
1. walks to school	✓			
2. drives to school				✓
3. is tired in the morning		✓		
4. is hungry around 11:00 a.m.			✓	

Sunita	Never	Sometimes	Often	Always
1. walks to school			✓	
2. drives to school		✓		
3. is tired in the morning				✓
4. is hungry around 11:00 a.m.	✓			

A John **never walks to school.** How about Sunita?

B She **often walks to school.**

USEFUL LANGUAGE
How about . . . ?
What about . . . ?

3 Communicate

A **Write.** Complete the sentences about yourself.

1. I am usually *hungry* around 11:00. I always *eat lunch* after class.
2. I am often ______ on Saturday.
3. I usually ______ during the summer.
4. I am never ______ in the afternoon.
5. I sometimes ______ late at night.
6. I always ______ on the weekend.
7. I rarely ______ in the morning.
8. I never ______ during the week.

B **Talk** with a partner. Use your answers from Exercise 3A.

I always eat lunch after class. What about you?

I always go to work after class.

Lesson D Reading

1 Before you read

Look at the picture. Answer the questions.

1. Who do you see in the picture?
2. Where is she?
3. What is she doing?

2 Read

Read the letter. Listen and read again.

CD 1, Track 38

New Message

Hi Layla,

Right now, my mother is visiting me here in Philadelphia. I rarely see her because she comes to Philadelphia only once a year. She usually stays for one month. Here is a photo of my mother at the airport last week. She was happy to see me!

This year, I want to take my mother to New York City. I want to show her the Statue of Liberty and Central Park. It takes about one and a half hours to get to New York by train. We are excited about our trip. Can you meet us there? I'm thinking around the end of March. Let me know.

Can't wait to see you!

Write me soon.

Binh

Capital letters can show you the names of cities or places.
New **Y**ork **C**ity
Statue of **L**iberty

3 After you read

Write. Correct the sentences.

1. Binh's mother comes to Philadelphia three times a year.
   Binh's mother comes to Philadelphia once a year.
2. Binh often sees his mother.
   ____
3. Binh wants to take his mother to Los Angeles.
   ____
4. Binh wants to show his mother the White House.
   ____
5. It takes two hours to get from Philadelphia to New York by train.
   ____

4 Picture dictionary Travel activities

1. write postcards

2. ____________

3. ____________

4. ____________

5. ____________

6. ____________

7. ____________

8. ____________

9. ____________

A **Write** the words in the Picture dictionary. Then listen and repeat.

buy souvenirs	go swimming	take a suitcase
go shopping	stay at a hotel	take pictures
go sightseeing	stay with relatives	write postcards

CD 1, Track 39

B **Talk** with a partner. Change the **bold** words and make conversations.

A Do you **write postcards** on a trip?
B Yes, I do. I always **write postcards**.

A Do you **stay at a hotel** on a trip?
B No, I don't. I never **stay at a hotel**.

For college and career readiness practice, see pages 144–145.

Identify the main idea and key details in an email about travel; use vocabulary for travel activities

Lesson E Writing

1 Before you write

A **Talk** with a partner. Ask and answer the questions.

1. When was your last trip?
2. Where did you go?
3. What did you do there?

B **Read** the letter from Alicia.

New Message

Hi, Margarita!

How are you? I just got back from a trip to Chicago. I went to visit my cousin, Isaac. Isaac lives in a suburb about one hour from Chicago called Aurora. I go to visit him once a year. It usually takes three hours to get there from Boston by plane.

This year we spent three days in the city of Chicago. We went sightseeing. I saw the Willis Tower, the tallest building in the United States. We also saw a concert in Millennium Park. We went shopping, and I bought souvenirs. It was a fun trip! Hope you are well. Write soon!

Your friend,

Alicia

C **Write.** Answer the questions about Alicia's letter. Write complete sentences.

1. Where did Alicia go? *Alicia went to Chicago.* __________
2. Who did she visit? __________
3. How often does she visit him? __________
4. How long does it usually take to get there? __________
____
5. What did she do there? __________
____
____

D **Write.** Answer the questions about yourself.

1. When was your last trip?

____

____

2. Where did you go?

____

____

3. How did you get there?

____

____

4. How often do you go there?

____

____

5. How long does it usually take to get there?

____

____

6. Who did you go with?

____

____

7. What did you do there?

____

____

USEFUL LANGUAGE

How did you get there?

By train.	*By bus.*
By plane.	*By car.*

2 Write

Write a letter to a friend about your last trip.
Use Exercises 1B and 1D to help you.

Spell out hours and minutes from one to ten:
***one** hour and **five** minutes*
Write all other times as numbers:
***11** hours and **30** minutes*

3 After you write

A **Read** your letter to a partner.

B **Check** your partner's letter.

- Where did your partner go?
- How long does it usually take to get there?
- Did your partner write the hours and minutes correctly?

Lesson F Another view

1 Life-skills reading

4:00 PM

Air American Flight Schedule

Flight	From	To	Departs	Arrives
Flight 885	Boston	New York	6:00 A.M.	7:35 A.M.
Flight 1005	Boston	New York	8:00 A.M.	9:09 A.M.
Flight 1007	Boston	New York	10:20 A.M.	11:30 A.M.
Flight 1009	Boston	New York	11:20 A.M.	12:35 P.M.
Flight 1015	Boston	New York	3:43 P.M.	5:00 P.M.
Flight 1017	Boston	New York	6:50 P.M.	8:18 P.M.

A **Read** the questions. Look at the airline schedule. Fill in the answer.

1. How long does it take to go to New York on Flight 1009?
   - (A) one hour
   - (B) one hour and five minutes
   - (C) one hour and ten minutes
   - (D) one hour and 15 minutes

2. How often do flights go from Boston to New York before 11:00 a.m.?
   - (A) once
   - (B) twice
   - (C) three times
   - (D) six times

3. Which statement is true?
   - (A) Flight 1015 arrives at about 3:30.
   - (B) Flight 1007 departs in the afternoon.
   - (C) Flight 885 leaves early.
   - (D) Flight 1007 arrives just after lunch.

4. How many flights arrive in New York after 11:00 a.m.?
   - (A) one
   - (B) two
   - (C) three
   - (D) four

B **Solve** the problem. Which solution is best? Circle your opinion.

Timothy is flying from Boston to New York to see his mother. The person next to him is asking him a lot of personal questions, such as, "Are you married? Where do you work?" Timothy doesn't know what to say. What should he do?

1. Say, "It's none of your business."
2. Answer the questions politely.
3. Say, "I'm sorry. I can't talk. I have work to do."
4. Other: ______________________

2 Grammar connections: the preposition to with movement

Use *to* to show movement. After *to* use a noun for a place. Before some nouns use *the*. Before other nouns, don't use *the*.

TO	*TO THE*	X (NO PREPOSITION)
class	airport	downtown
Chicago	bank	outside
church	bus stop	overseas
school	library	somewhere
work	shopping mall	upstairs

Watch

A **Talk** with a partner. Answer the question with a place. Use *to*, *to the*, or place without *to* or *to the*.

1. **A** Where do the students go from Monday to Friday?
   B They ____________

2. **A** Where does Jack go from Monday to Friday?
   B He ____________

3. **A** Where does Alexia go to use a computer?
   B She ____________

4. **A** Where are the students going to meet for lunch?
   B ____________

5. **A** Where do the employees go every morning?
   B ____________

6. **A** Where is Fatima going?
   B ____________

B **Talk** with a partner. Ask each other the questions. Answer in complete sentences.

1. Where do you go to borrow a book?
2. Where do you go to wait for the bus?
3. Where do you go to study English?
4. Where do you sometimes go on Sunday?
5. Where should I go to find a museum or government office?

Scan an airline schedule for key details; use the preposition to with movement

UNIT 6 TIME

Lesson A Listening

1 Before you listen

A Look at the picture. What do you see?

B Point to: ■ a class picture ■ a family picture ■ a photo album ■ a baby picture ■ a graduation picture ■ a wedding picture

C Look at the people. What are they doing?

UNIT GOALS
Recall events from own life **Read** and complete timelines
Interpret information on an application

2 Listen

A **Listen.** What is Olga talking about? Write the letter of the conversation.

CD 2, Track 2

1. ____

2. ____

3. ____

B **Listen again.** Write *T* (true) or *F* (false).

CD 2, Track 2

Conversation A

1. Olga moved into her apartment two months ago. T
2. Olga got married in 2003. ____
3. Victoria got married 30 years ago. ____

Conversation B

4. Sergey is 14. ____
5. Sergey started college in September. ____
6. Natalya started college on Tuesday. ____

Conversation C

7. Olga met her husband in Moscow. ____
8. Olga moved to Russia about 14 years ago. ____
9. Natalya was born in Russia. ____

Listen again. Check your answers. Correct the false statements.

3 After you listen

Talk with a partner. Ask and answer the questions.

1. When do children start high school and college in countries you know?
2. At what age do people get married in countries you know?
3. When do people usually start their first jobs?

Lesson B When did you move here?

1 Grammar focus: *When* questions and simple past

Use *when* to ask about time. Use *did* + the base form of the verb to make a simple past question.

QUESTIONS			ANSWERS	
When did	you / he / she / they	**move** here?	I / He / she / They	**moved** here in July.

Regular verbs

finish → finished
graduate → graduated
start → started
study → studied

Irregular verbs

begin → began
find → found
get → got
have → had
leave → left
meet → met

Watch

2 Practice

A **Write.** Complete the conversations. Use the simple past.

1. **A** When ___did___ Min leave South Korea?
   B She ___left___ South Korea in 2014.
   A When ______ she move to New York?
   B She ______ to New York in 2016.
2. **A** When ______ Carlos start school?
   B He ______ school in September.
   A When ______ he graduate?
   B He ______ in June.
3. **A** When ______ Paul and Amy meet?
   B They ______ in 2014.
   A When ______ they get married?
   B They ______ married in 2017.
4. **A** When ______ you ______ college?
   B I finished college in August.
   A When ______ you get your first job?
   B I ______ my first job in September.

Listen and repeat. Then practice with a partner.

CD 2, Track 3

B **Read** Kasem's and Nee's time lines.

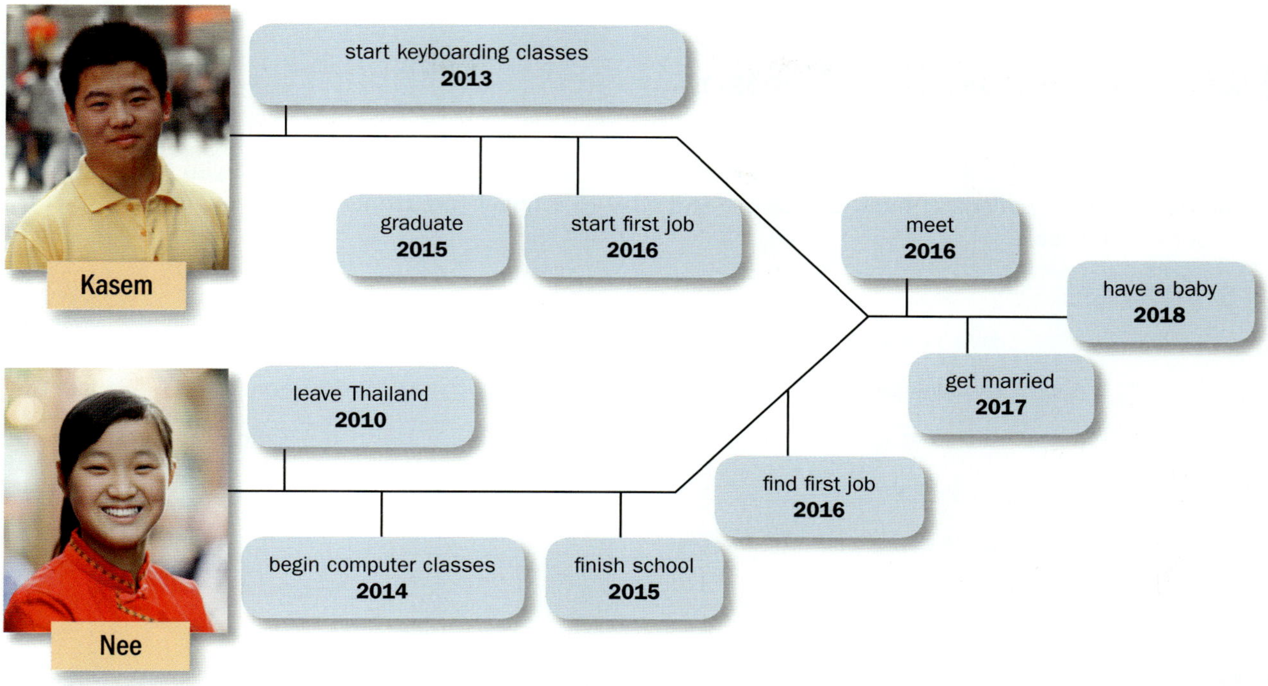

Talk with a partner. Change the bold words and make conversations.

A When did **Kasem start keyboarding classes**?
B **He started keyboarding classes** in **2013**.

1. Kasem / start keyboarding classes
2. Nee / begin computer classes
3. Kasem / graduate
4. Kasem and Nee / meet
5. Nee / find her first job
6. Kasem and Nee / have a baby
7. Nee / finish school
8. Kasem and Nee / get married
9. Nee / leave Thailand
10. Kasem / start his first job

3 Communicate

Talk with a partner. Complete the chart.

A Ali, when did you start English classes?
B I started English classes in 2017.

start English classes	*in 2017*
move to this country	
start your first job	

Lesson C He graduated two years ago.

1 Grammar focus: time phrases

Use *at* with time. Use *in* with months and years. Use *on* with days and dates. Use *ago* with phrases for past periods of time. Use *before* and *after* to connect two events and show the order of the events.

STATEMENTS			
He graduated	two years ago.	She got married	at 3:00 p.m.
	two weeks ago.		at 12:00 noon.
	in May.		before she came to the U.S.
	in 2014.		after she came to the U.S.
	on Wednesday.		last year.
	on May 4th, 2014.		this week.

Watch

2 Practice

A **Write.** Complete the conversations. Use *at, in, on,* or *ago*.

1. **A** When did Lou and Angela buy their new car?
   B They bought their new car ___three weeks ago___. (three weeks)
2. **A** When did Lou and Angela get married?
   B They got married ______________. (four years)
3. **A** When did Angela have a baby?
   B She had a baby yesterday ______________. (8:20 a.m.)
4. **A** When did Lou begin his new job?
   B He began his new job ______________. (Tuesday)
5. **A** When did Lou move to the United States?
   B He moved to the United States ______________. (December 15th)
6. **A** When did Angela come to the United States?
   B She came to the United States ______________. (five years)
7. **A** When did Angela take the citizenship exam?
   B She took the citizenship exam ______________. (March)
8. **A** When did Angela register to vote?
   B She registered to vote ______________. (June)

CULTURE NOTE
The citizenship exam is a test you have to take to become an American citizen.

Listen and repeat. Then practice with a partner.

CD 2, Track 4

B Write. Complete the sentences. Use *at*, *in*, or *on*.

1. Anna graduated ___in___ 2005.

2. She got married ______ Saturday, August 16th, 2008.

3. She had a baby ______ June 21st, 2011, ______ 2:30 a.m.

4. She and her family moved to the United States ______ 2012.

5. She and her husband bought a house ______ April.

6. Anna took the citizenship exam ______ May 16th.

7. She became a citizen ______ Thursday.

8. She started her new job yesterday ______ 9:00 a.m.

Talk with a partner. Change the **bold** words and make conversations. Use *before* or *after*.

A When did Anna **graduate**?
B She **graduated before** she moved to the United States.

1. graduate
2. buy a house
3. become a citizen
4. get married
5. take the citizenship exam
6. have a baby

3 Communicate

Read. What did you do? Check (✓) the boxes.

- ☐ get married
- ☐ have a baby
- ☐ get a driver's license
- ☐ get a new job
- ☐ register for English class
- ☐ buy a car
- ☐ move here
- ☐ study computers

USEFUL LANGUAGE
I'm not married.
I don't have any children.
I didn't study computers.

Talk with a partner. Ask and answer questions.

When did you get married?

I got married three years ago on August 25th.

Lesson D Reading

1 Before you read

Look at the picture. Answer the questions.

1. Who are the people?
2. Where are they?
3. What are they doing?

2 Read

Read the interview. Listen and read again.

CD 2, Track 5

An Interesting Life

Interviewer: What happened after you graduated from high school?

Olga: I went to university in Moscow, and I met my husband there. It was a long time ago! We were in the same class. We fell in love and got married on April 2nd, 2000. We had a small wedding in Moscow.

Interviewer: What happened after you got married?

Olga: I finished university and found a job. I was a teacher. Then, I had a baby. My husband and I were very excited to have a little boy.

Interviewer: When did you move to the United States?

Olga: We immigrated about 14 years ago. We became American citizens eight years ago.

Skim: Read the questions. They tell you the focus of the interview.

3 After you read

A **Write.** Answer the questions about Olga. Write complete sentences.

1. What is the focus of the interview? *The focus is Olga's life.*
2. When did Olga meet her husband? ____________
3. When did they become American citizens? ____________
4. When did she and her family move to the U.S.? ____________
5. Reread the interview. What makes Olga's life interesting? Use evidence from the interview.

____

B **Number** the sentences in the correct order.

____ Olga had a baby boy.

____ She moved to the U.S.

____ She found a job.

____ Olga got married.

____ She met her husband.

____ She became a U.S. citizen.

__1__ Olga graduated from high school.

____ Olga finished university.

4 Picture dictionary Life events

1. retired

2. ______________

3. ______________

4. ______________

5. ______________

6. ______________

7. ______________

8. ______________

9. ______________

A **Write** the words in the Picture dictionary. Then listen and repeat.

fell in love	got divorced	got engaged	got married	got promoted
had a baby	immigrated	retired	started a business	

CD 2, Track 6

B **Talk** with a partner. Which life events happened to you? When did they happen? What happened after that?

I retired two years ago. After I retired, I started English classes.

For college and career readiness practice, see pages 146–147.

Identify the main idea and key details in an interview about a person's life; use vocabulary for life events

Lesson E Writing

1 Before you write

A **Talk** with a partner. Ask and answer the questions.

1. What three events were important in your life?
2. When was each event?

Write. Make a time line. Use your partner's information.

My partner's time line

1 ______________ 2 ______________ 3 ______________

B **Read** about Bo-hai in his company newsletter.

COMPUTER SYSTEMS INC.

A New Employee: Bo-hai Cheng

I was born in 1994 in Beijing. I started university in 2012. I studied civil engineering. In 2015, I moved to Miami. After I moved, I bought a car. I also got engaged. Then I studied computers at a vocational school. I graduated on July 3rd. Three weeks ago, I found a computer job. In October, I'm going to get married!

C **Write.** Complete Bo-hai's time line.

bought a car	found a job	graduated from vocational school
moved to Miami	started university	was born in 1994

Bo-hai's time line

1 *was born in 1994*

2 ______________

3 ______________

4 ______________

5 ______________

6 ______________

D **Write** each sentence a different way.

1. I started change college to university in 2012.
   In 2012, I started change college to university.
2. In 2015, I moved to Miami.
   ____
3. I graduated on July 3rd.
   ____
4. Three weeks ago, I found a computer job.
   ____
5. In October, I'm going to get married.
   ____

Use a comma (,) after time phrases like *In 2012* or *On July 3rd* at the beginning of a sentence.

E **Write.** Complete the time line about yourself.

My time line

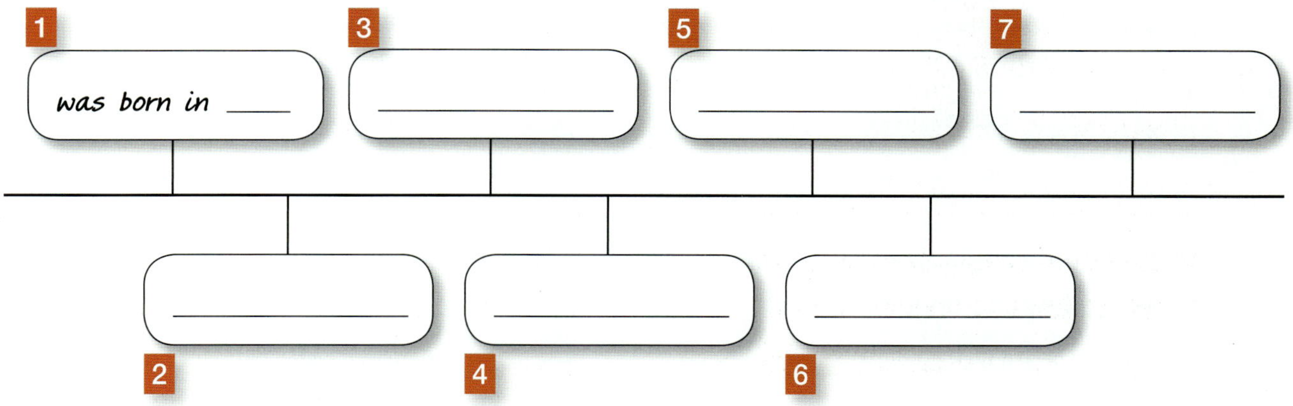

2 Write

Write a paragraph about yourself. Use Exercises 1B and 1E to help you.

3 After you write

A **Read** your paragraph to a partner.

B **Check** your partner's paragraph.

- What are the important events?
- What time phrases are in the paragraph?
- Are there commas after time phrases at the beginning of sentences?

Lesson F Another view

1 Life-skills reading

www.webaddress.com

APPLICATION FOR A MARRIAGE LICENSE

Groom's Personal Data

1A. Name of Groom (First)	1B. Middle	1C. Last	2. Birthdate (Mo / Day / Yr)
Antonio	Marco	Velez	06/12/1990

3A. Residence (Street & Number)	3B. City	3C. Zip Code	3D. State	4. Place of Birth
406 E. 37th Street	Austin	78705	TX	Mexico City, Mexico

5. Number of Previous Marriages	6A. Last Marriage Ended by	6B. Date (Mo / Day / Yr)
1	Divorce	08/13/2014

Bride's Personal Data

1A. Name of Bride (First)	1B. Middle	1C. Last	2. Birthdate (Mo / Day / Yr)
Maria	Luisa	Camacho	11/17/1995

3A. Residence (Street & Number)	3B. City	3C. Zip Code	3D. State	4. Place of Birth
1005 Hillside Oaks Drive	Austin	78710	TX	Lima, Peru

5. Number of Previous Marriages	6A. Last Marriage Ended by	6B. Date (Mo / Day / Yr)
None		

Groom's Driver's License / I.D.#:	Bride's Driver's License / I.D.#:
C0581316429	C0901516531
Ceremony Date:	**Ceremony Location:**
June 22, 2018	City Hall

A **Read** the questions. Look at the application for a marriage license. Fill in the answer.

1. When was the bride born?
   - (A) in 1990
   - (B) in 1995
   - (C) in 1994
   - (D) in 2014

2. What phrase on the application is a clue to the meaning of *divorce*?
   - (A) marriage date
   - (B) ceremony date
   - (C) ceremony location
   - (D) marriage ended

3. Which statement is true?
   - (A) Antonio was married before.
   - (B) Maria was married before.
   - (C) Antonio is from Peru.
   - (D) Maria is from Mexico.

4. When is their wedding ceremony?
   - (A) on 6/12/90
   - (B) on 8/13/14
   - (C) on 2/6/18
   - (D) on 6/22/18

B **Solve** the problem. Which solution is best? Circle your opinion.

Tony is going to get his marriage license today. He knows he has to take identification. Last night someone stole his wallet, so he doesn't have a driver's license. What should he do?

1. Go to the appointment.
2. Wait for a new driver's license.
3. Call the Department of Motor Vehicles.
4. Other: ______________________

2 Grammar connections: *someone, some, anyone, everyone,* and *no one*

Use *someone, some, everyone,* and *no one* when you don't know who or don't say who.
Use *anyone* in the question.

QUESTION	ANSWERS	CLASS INFORMATION
Is **anyone** from Haiti?	Yes, **someone** is from Haiti. *someone* = one person	Lisette – Haiti Cesar – Mexico
	No, **no one** is from Haiti. *no one* = no people	Cesar – Mexico Boris – Russia
	Yes, **everyone** is from Haiti. *everyone* = all people	Lisette – Haiti Ines – Haiti Franz– Haiti
	Yes, **some** are from Haiti. *some* = a few people	Lisette – Haiti Ines – Haiti Cesar – Mexico

Watch

A **Work** in a group. Complete the chart.

A: Are you married, Lisette?
B: Yes, I am.

A Are you playing the piano?
B No, I don't.

	______ (name)	______ (name)	______ (name)
1. Are you married?			
2. Are you single?			
3. Do you have children?			
4. Do you have a brother?			
5. Do you have a sister?			
6. Do you have grandchildren?			
7. Do you have a middle name?			

B **Share** your group's information with another group.

In our group, everyone is married. No one is single . . .

Scan an application for key details; contrast *someone, some, anyone, everyone,* and *no one*

REVIEW

1 Listening

Read the questions. Then listen and circle the answers.

CD 2, Track 7

1. Where are Pablo and Marie?
   a. at a bus station
   (b.) at an airport
2. Why is Marie there?
   a. She just came back from Florida.
   b. She is meeting her parents.
3. How often does Marie visit her parents?
   a. every three months
   b. three times a year
4. Why is Pablo there?
   a. to meet Marie
   b. to meet his brother
5. How often does David visit?
   a. every weekend
   b. every vacation
6. How long does David usually stay?
   a. for three days
   b. for a week

Talk with a partner. Ask and answer the questions. Use complete sentences.

2 Grammar

A **Write.** Complete the story.

CHRISTINA'S LAST VACATION

Twice a year, Christina *takes* (1. take) a two-week vacation. Last year, she ________ (2. visit) her brother in New York City. It ________ (3. take) two days to get there by train. She and her brother ________ (4. see) a baseball game at Yankee Stadium and ________ (5. go) to a concert in Central Park. It ________ (6. be) a great vacation. Christina always ________ (7. have) a good time with her brother.

B **Write.** Look at the answers. Write the questions.

1. **A** How often *does Christina take a vacation*?
   B Christina takes a vacation twice a year.
2. **A** When ________________
   B She visited her brother in New York City last year.
3. **A** How long ________________?
   B It took two days to get there.
4. **A** Where ________________?
   B They saw a baseball game at Yankee Stadium.

Talk with a partner. Ask and answer the questions.

3 Pronunciation: intonation in questions

A **Listen** to the intonation in these questions.

Where is the train station?

Is the train station on Broadway or on Main Street?

CD 2, Track 8

B **Listen and repeat.**

Wh- questions

C How often do you eat at a restaurant?

B Once a week.

Or questions

A Do you eat at a restaurant once a week or once a month?

B Once a week.

CD 2, Track 9

C **Talk** with a partner. Ask and answer the questions.

1. How often do you take a vacation?
2. Do you like to take a vacation in the summer or in the winter?
3. When was your last vacation?
4. Where did you go?
5. Did you go alone or with your family?
6. What did you do there?

D **Write** six questions. Make at least three questions using *or*.

1.
2.
3.
4.
5.
6.

Talk with a partner. Ask and answer the questions.

Do you take a bus or a train to school?

I take a bus.

UNIT 7 SHOPPING

Lesson A Listening

1 Before you listen

A Look at the picture. What do you see?

B Point to: ■ a customer ■ a piano ■ appliances ■ a sofa ■ furniture ■ a price tag ■ a salesperson ■ a stove

C Describe the furniture. How much do the items cost?

2 Listen

A **Listen.** What are Nick and Denise talking about? Write the letter of the conversation.

CD2, Track 10

1. ____

2. ____

3. ____

B **Listen again.** Write *T* (true) or *F* (false).

CD2, Track 10

Conversation A

1. Denise and Nick need furniture. T
2. Denise and Nick bought a house two days ago. ____
3. Only the furniture is marked down 20 percent. ____

Conversation B

4. Denise likes the brown sofa. ____
5. Nick wants a big sofa. ____
6. Denise likes the blue sofa. ____

Conversation C

7. Denise and Nick need a piano. ____
8. The upright piano is very old. ____
9. The sound of the smaller piano is better. ____

Listen again. Check your answers. Correct the false statements.

3 After you listen

Talk with a partner. Ask and answer the questions.

1. What are some good ways to find furniture?
2. Did you ever buy furniture in this country?
3. What did you buy?

CULTURE NOTE
Some stores in the U.S. sell furniture and appliances that are not new. They are called *secondhand*, *thrift*, or *consignment* stores. Their prices are cheaper.

Lesson B The blue sofa is smaller.

1 Grammar focus: comparatives

Use comparative adjectives to compare two things.

TYPE OF ADJECTIVE	COMPARATIVE	EXAMPLE	
one syllable	add *er*	cheap – cheaper tall – taller	big – bigger wide – wider
two or more syllables	use *more*	comfortable – more comfortable expensive – more expensive	
ending in *y*	change *y* to *ier*	heavy – heavier pretty – prettier	
irregular		good – better	bad – worse

Watch

QUESTIONS	ANSWERS
Which sofa is **smaller**?	The blue sofa is **smaller**.
Which sofa is **more expensive**?	The white sofa is **more expensive**.

2 Practice

A Write. Complete the conversations. Use comparatives.

1. **A** Which chair is ___heavier___? (heavy)

   B ___The orange chair is heavier.___
   (orange chair / purple chair)

2. **A** Which refrigerator is ____________? (expensive)

   B ____________________________
   (small refrigerator / large refrigerator)

3. **A** Which table is ____________? (big)

   B ____________________________
   (square table / round table)

4. **A** Which stove is ____________? (good)

   B ____________________________
   (white stove / black stove)

5. **A** Which lamp is ____________? (tall)

   B ____________________________
   (floor lamp / table lamp)

6. **A** Which sofa is ____________? (comfortable)

   B ____________________________
   (green striped sofa / blue plaid sofa)

1.

2.

3.

4.

5.

6.

Listen and repeat. Then practice with a partner.

CD2, Track 11

B **Talk** with a partner. Change the **bold** words and make conversations.

dining table

kitchen table

desk lamp

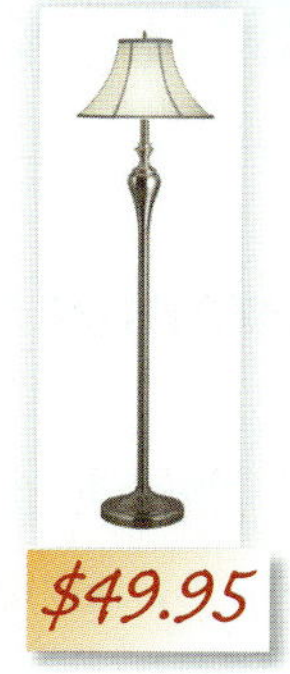

floor lamp

A Which **table** is **heavier**?
B The **dining table** is **heavier**.

1. table / heavy
2. table / small
3. table / expensive
4. table / tall
5. table / wide
6. lamp / short
7. lamp / beautiful
8. lamp / cheap
9. lamp / good
10. lamp / large

USEFUL LANGUAGE
The dining table is heavier.
The dining table is heavier than the kitchen table.

3 Communicate

Talk with a partner. Compare the furniture in each store window.

A I like the **lamp** at **Perry's Thrift Shop**.
B Why?
A It's **prettier**.

Lesson C The yellow chair is the cheapest.

1 Grammar focus: superlatives

Use superlative adjectives to compare three or more things.

TYPE OF ADJECTIVE	SUPERLATIVE	EXAMPLE	
one syllable	use *the* and add *-est*	cheap – the cheapest big – the biggest	tall – the tallest wide – the widest
two or more syllables	use *the most*	comfortable – the most comfortable expensive – the most expensive	
ending in *y*	use *the* and change *y* to *ier*	heavy – the heaviest pretty – the prettiest	
irregular		good – the best	bad – the worst

Watch

STATEMENTS
The blue chair is **cheap**.
The red chair is **cheaper**
The yellow chair is **the cheapest**.

2 Practice

A Write. Complete the conversations. Use superlatives.

1. **A** Which TV is *the cheapest*? (cheap)
   B *The second TV is the cheapest.*
2. **A** Which TV is ____________? (heavy)
   B ____________
3. **A** Which TV is ____________? (expensive)
   B ____________
4. **A** Which TV is ____________? (old)
   B ____________
5. **A** Which TV is ____________? (small)
   B ____________
6. **A** Which TV is ____________? (wide)
   B ____________
7. **A** Which TV is ____________? (good)
   B ____________
8. **A** Which TV is ____________? (new)
   B ____________

Listen and repeat. Then practice with a partner.

CD2, Track 12

B **Write.** Complete the conversation. Use superlatives.

A This is ___the newest___ (1. new) shopping mall in the city. It's great.

B Where's ______ (2. good) place to buy clothes?

A Well, there are three clothing stores. Mega Store is ______ (3. big) one.

It usually has ______ (4. low) prices, but it's ______ (5. crowded). I never go there.

B What about Cleo's Boutique?

A Cleo's Boutique is ______ (6. beautiful) store. It's nice, but it's ______ (7. expensive).

B What about Madison's?

A Well, it's ______ (8. small), but it's my favorite. It has ______ (9. nice) clothes and ______ (10. friendly) salespeople.

B Look! Madison's is having a big sale. Let's go!

> **USEFUL LANGUAGE**
> It has low prices.
> It has cheap prices.

Listen and check your answers. Then practice with a partner.

CD2, Track 13

3 Communicate

Talk in a group. Ask and answer the questions about places in your community.

1. Which clothing store is the biggest?
2. Which clothing store has the lowest prices?
3. Which supermarket is the cheapest?
4. Which restaurant is the best?

Lesson D Reading

1 Before you read

Look at the picture. Answer the questions.

1. Who is the woman?
2. What did she buy?

2 Read

Read the newspaper article. Listen and read again.

CD2, Track 14

Today's Question

What's the best thing you ever bought?

The best thing I ever bought was an old piano. I bought it in a used-furniture store last month. It was the most beautiful piano in the store, but it wasn't very expensive. It has a beautiful sound. Now my two children are taking piano lessons. I love to hear music in the house.

Denise Robinson
Charleston, SC

I bought a used van five years ago. I used my van to help people move and to deliver stoves and refrigerators from a secondhand appliance store. I made a lot of money with that van. Now I have my own business. That van is the best thing I ever bought.

Sammy Chin
Myrtle Beach, SC

guess the meaning of new words from other words nearby.
piano – music

3 After you read

Write. Answer the questions about the article. Write complete sentences.

1. What question are Denise and Sammy answering?
   They are answering the question, "What's the best thing you ever bought?"
2. What did Sammy buy? ______
3. Who is taking piano lessons? ______
4. Who has a business? ______
5. What words in the reading help you understand the word *appliances*? ______
6. Did Sammy have a lot of money five years ago? Why do you think so? ______

4 Picture dictionary Furniture

A **Write** the words in the Picture dictionary. Then listen and repeat.

aquarium	coffee table	end table	mirror	sofa bed
bookcase	computer desk	entertainment center	recliner	

CD2, Track 15

B **Talk** with a partner. Change the **bold** words and make conversations.

A Which is **bigger**, the **coffee table** or the **end table**?
B The **coffee table** is **bigger**.

A Do you like the **bookcase**?
B **Yes, I do.** It's **nicer** than my **bookcase**.

For college and career readiness practice, see pages 148–149.

Identify the topic and key details of an article about purchases; use vocabulary for furniture

Lesson E Writing

1 Before you write

A **Talk** with a partner. These items are gifts. Which gift is the best? Tell why.

1.

2.

3.

B **Talk** with three classmates. Ask questions and complete the chart.

1. What's the best gift you ever received?
2. Who gave it to you?
3. When did you receive this gift?
4. Why was it the best gift?

Name	Paolo			
Best gift	*a trip to Brazil*			
From	*his wife*			
When	*last summer*			
Why	*because he saw his parents again*			

Talk. Share your information with the class.

Paolo's best gift was a trip to Brazil last summer. His wife gave it to him. It was the best gift because he saw his parents again.

C **Read** the story. Complete the sentences.

ago	heart	necklace
birthday	mother	store

The Best Gift

The best gift I ever received was a ___necklace___(1).

My ________(2) bought it in a jewelry ________(3).

The necklace was in the shape of a ________(4).

She gave it to me for my ________(5) a long

time ________(6). My mother said it was her heart.

It was the best gift because it was from her.

D **Write.** Answer the questions about yourself.

1. What is the best gift you ever received? ____________________
2. Who gave it to you? ____________________
3. Where did the gift come from? ____________________
4. When did you receive this gift? ____________________
5. Why was it the best gift? ____________________

2 Write

Write a paragraph about the best gift you ever received. Use Exercises 1C and 1D to help you.

Use *because* to answer the question *Why* and to give a reason.
*It was the best gift **because** it was beautiful.*

3 After you write

A **Read** your paragraph to a partner.

B **Check** your partner's paragraph.

- What was the gift?
- Why was it the best gift?
- Did your partner use *because* to say why?

Lesson F Another view

1 Life-skills reading

SALES RECEIPT

	Al's Discount Furniture 2100 Willow Boulevard Charleston, SC 29401 (843) 555-0936	**Sold to:** Nick Robinson 2718 Central Avenue Charleston, SC 29412
Item #	**Description**	**Price**
1.	Green sofa	$699.00
2.	Coffee table	$295.00
3.	Table lamp	$39.95
4.	Bookcase	$149.00
	Subtotal Sales tax 8.5%	$1,182.95 $100.55
	TOTAL	**$1,283.50**
	VISTA/MASTER CHARGE	$1,283.50

No refunds or exchanges after 30 days.

A **Read** the questions. Look at the sales receipt. Fill in the answer.

1. Which is the cheapest item?
   - (A) the green sofa
   - (B) the bookcase
   - (C) the coffee table
   - (D) the table lamp

2. Which word in the receipt means *money back*?
   - (A) Discount
   - (B) refunds
   - (C) exchanges
   - (D) Subtotal

3. When can a customer not exchange an item?
   - (A) after 7 days
   - (B) after 15 days
   - (C) after 30 days
   - (D) before 30 days

4. Which statement is true?
   - (A) The total is $1,182.95.
   - (B) The coffee table is cheaper than the bookcase.
   - (C) The customer bought four items.
   - (D) The sales tax is 8%.

B **Solve** the problem. Which solution is best? Circle your opinion.

Tony bought a bookcase at Al's Discount Furniture. When he got home, the bookcase was too large for his room. Tony wants to exchange the bookcase for a smaller bookcase, but he can't find his receipt. What should he do?

1. Take the bookcase back to the store.
2. Call the store and ask for the sales clerk.
3. Give the bookcase to his friend.
4. Other: ______________________

2 Grammar connections: *one, the other, some, the others*

The pronouns *one, the other, some,* and *the others* can replace nouns.

There are two shoe stores.

{One shoe store / **One**} has men's shoes, and {the other shoe store / **the other**} has women's shoes.

There are many restaurants.

{Some restaurants / **Some**} have fast food, and {the other restaurants / **the others**} have international food.

Watch

A **Work with a partner.** Look at the stores in a mall directory. Talk about what they have. Take turns.

A There are two shoe stores.

B Yes. *One* has men's shoes, and *the other* has women's shoes. There are five restaurants in the food court.

A Yes. *Some* have fast food, and *the others* have international food.

DIRECTORY OF STORES

SHOE STORES
- **Men's**: The Shoe Place
- **Women's**: Shoe Time

CLOTHING STORES
- **Women's**: Victoria Dresses, California Style
- **Men's**: Jack's Jeans, The Modern Man

HOUSEWARE STORES
- **Kitchen**: Ned's Kitchen
- **Bed and Bath**: Home Touch

ELECTRONICS STORES
- **Computers**: Computer Center, T-Plus
- **Wireless**: Horizon Phones, Mega Metro Phones

FURNITURE STORES
- Beautiful Bedrooms
- Sofa World

FOOD COURT
- **Fast Food**: Chicken-To-Go, Fast and Now, Sandwich Plus
- **International Food**: Food Palace, Pasta House

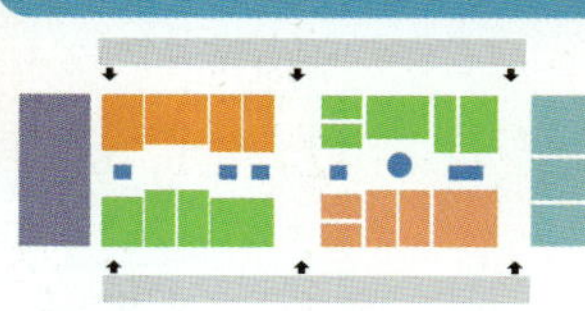

B **Work with your partner.** Look at the picture. Make sentences with *one, the other, some,* and *the others*.

There are two dresses. One is red, and the other is black.

Yes, and one is long, and the other is short.

Scan a sales receipt for key information; contrast *one, the other, some,* and *the others*

UNIT 8 WORK

Lesson A Listening

1 Before you listen

A Look at the picture. What do you see?

B Point to: ■ a lab ■ linens ■ a patient ■ a walker supplies ■ co-workers ■ an orderly ■ a wheelchair

C Look at these people. What are they doing?

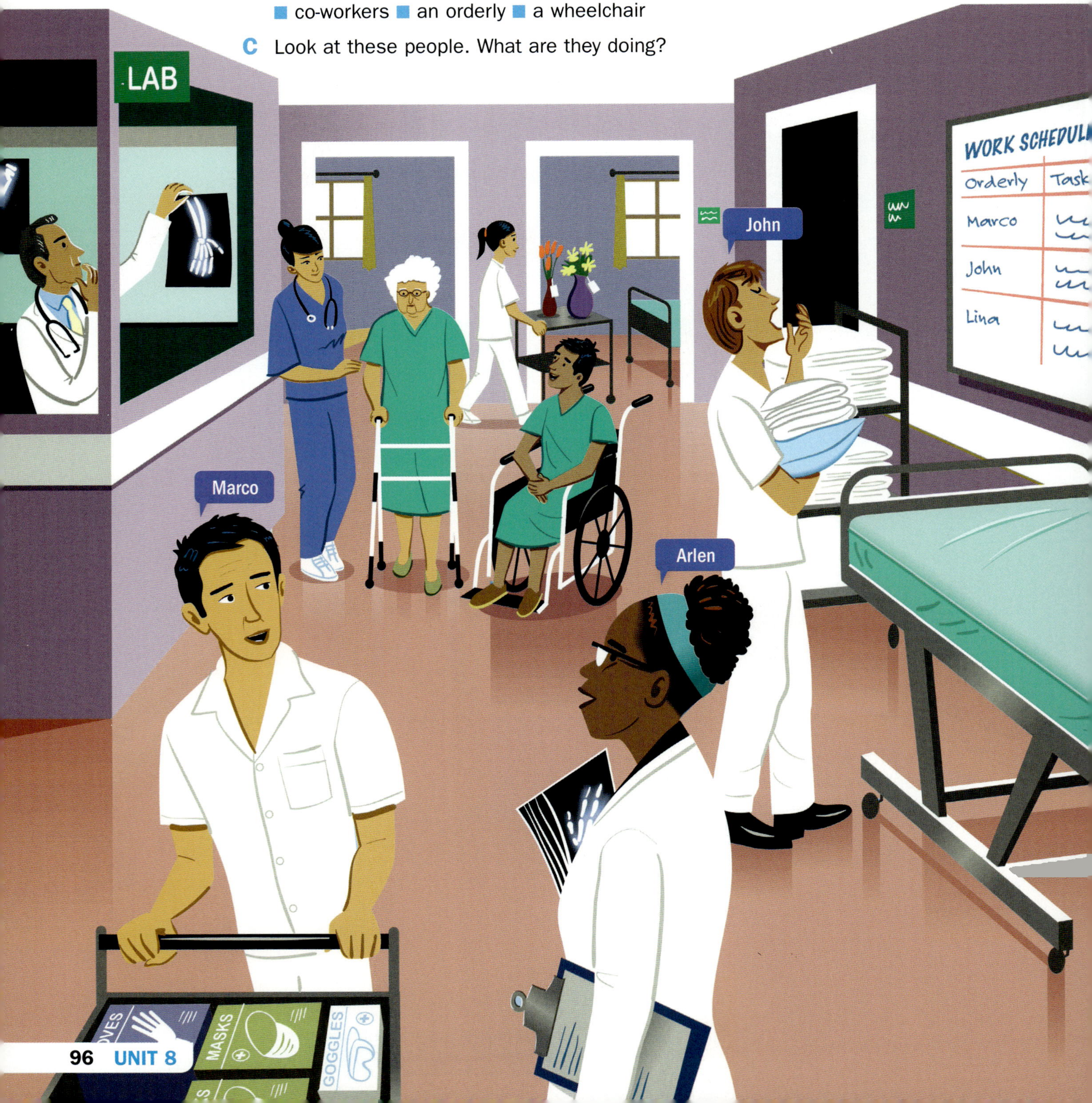

UNIT GOALS
Describe job duties **Describe** past activities
Interpret information on a weekly time sheet

2 Listen

A **Listen.** What is Marco talking about? Write the letter of the conversation.

CD2, Track 16

1. ____

2. ____

3. ____

B **Listen again.** Write *T* (true) or *F* (false).

CD2, Track 16

Conversation A

1. Marco picked up X-rays this morning. __T__
2. Marco delivered linens to the third floor. ____
3. Marco needs to prepare rooms on the second floor. ____

Conversation B

4. John is tired. ____
5. Marco worked the night shift. ____
6. Marco wants to go back to school. ____

Conversation C

7. Suzanne works in Human Resources. ____
8. Marco wants to be a nurse. ____
9. Marco wants to work full-time. ____

Listen again. Check your answers. Correct the false statements.

CULTURE NOTE
People who work at night work the night shift.

3 After you listen

Talk with a partner. Ask and answer the questions.

1. Do you have a job? What do you do?
2. Did you have a job before? What did you do?
3. What job do you want in the future?

Lesson B Where did you go last night?

1 Grammar focus: *What* and *Where* questions and simple past

Use *what* to ask about activities. Use *where* to ask about location.

QUESTIONS			ANSWERS	
What did	you	**do** yesterday?	I	**worked.**
	he		He	
	they		They	
Where did	you	**go** last night?	I	**went** to a meeting.
	she		She	
	they		They	

Regular verbs

clean → cleaned
deliver → delivered
help → helped
pick up → picked up
prepare → prepared

Irregular verbs

go → went
make → made
meet → met
take → took

Watch

2 Practice

A **Write.** Complete the conversations. Use *What* or *Where* and the simple past.

1. **A** ___What___ did Linda do after breakfast?
   B She ___made___ (make) the beds.
2. **A** ____________ did Brenda and Leo do this morning?
   B They ____________ (pick up) patients in the reception area.
3. **A** ____________ did Trevor do this morning?
   B He ____________ (deliver) X-rays.
4. **A** ____________ did Jill and Brad take the linens?
   B They ____________ (take) the linens to the second floor.
5. **A** ____________ did Felix do yesterday?
   B He ____________ (help) patients with their walkers and wheelchairs.
6. **A** ____________ did Juan and Ivana go after work?
   B They ____________ (go) to the coffee shop across the street.
7. **A** ____________ did Marco do after lunch?
   B He ____________ (prepare) the rooms on the 2nd floor.
8. **A** ____________ did Suzanne meet Marco?
   B She ____________ (meet) him in her office.

Listen and repeat. Then practice with a partner.

CD2, Track 17

B **Talk** with a partner. Change the **bold** words and make conversations.

A Where did Rosa go at **8:00**?
B She went to the **coffee shop**.
A What did she do there?
B She **ate breakfast**.

Rosa's schedule

8:00	*eat breakfast at the coffee shop ✓*
9:30	*prepare rooms on the fourth floor ✓*
10:30	*meet patients in the reception area ✓*
11:30	*pick up X-rays from the lab ✓*
1:00	*meet Amy in the cafeteria ✓*
2:00	*clean the furniture in the reception area ✓*
3:00	*make the beds on the first floor ✓*
3:30	*deliver supplies to the third floor ✓*
4:30	*pick up X-rays from the lab ✓*
5:30	*go to English class at the community college ✓*

3 Communicate

Talk with a partner. Ask questions. Write your partner's answers in the chart.

A Rachel, where did you go last weekend?
B I went to the mall.
A What did you do?
B I ate lunch and went shopping.
A Did you have fun?
B Yes, I did.

	Where?	What?
last weekend	*the mall*	*ate lunch and went shopping*
last Monday		
this morning		
last summer		
last night		

Lesson C I work on Saturdays and Sundays.

1 Grammar focus: conjunctions *and*, *or*, *but*

Use *and*, *or* or *but* to connect words, phrases and sentences. Use *and* to connect similar ideas. Use *or* to connect choices. Use *but* to connect different ideas.

STATEMENTS		
I work on Saturdays. I also work on Sundays.	}	I work on Saturdays **and** Sundays.
Sometimes he works on Saturdays. Sometimes he works on Sundays.	}	He works on Saturdays **or** Sundays.
She works on Saturdays. She doesn't work on Sundays.	}	She works on Saturdays, **but** she doesn't work on Sundays.

Watch

2 Practice

A Write. Combine the sentences. Use *and*, *or*, or *but*.

1. Sometimes Irene eats Chinese food for lunch. Sometimes she eats Mexican food for lunch.
   Irene eats Chinese or Mexican food for lunch.
2. Tito works the day shift. Tito also works the night shift.
   ____
3. Marco had an interview. He didn't get the job.
   ____
4. Brian likes his co-workers. He doesn't like his schedule.
   ____
5. Erica takes care of her children. She also takes care of her grandmother.
   ____
6. Carl cleaned the carpets. He didn't make the beds.
   ____
7. Sometimes Kate works in Austin. Sometimes she works in Houston.
   ____
8. Ilya speaks Russian at home. He also speaks Russian at work.
   ____

Listen and repeat. Check your answers.

CD2, Track 18

B **Talk** with a partner. Change the bold words and make conversations. Use *and*, *but* or *or*.

A What did Ahmed do this morning?
B He **wrote reports** and **checked email**.

1.

write reports / check email

2.

make copies / deliver mail

3.

answer calls / take messages

A What did Jill do yesterday?
B She **went to work,** but she **didn't feel well**.

4.

go to work / feel well

5.

go to a meeting / take notes

6.

write a letter / finish it

A Where do you eat lunch?
B I eat lunch **in a restaurant** or **at my desk**.

7.

in a restaurant / at my desk

8.

in the cafeteria / outside

9.

at home / in my car

3 Communicate

Talk with a partner. Make statements with *and*, *or*, or *but*.

Last night, I watched TV and did my homework. What about you?

I did my homework, but I didn't watch TV.

Lesson D Reading

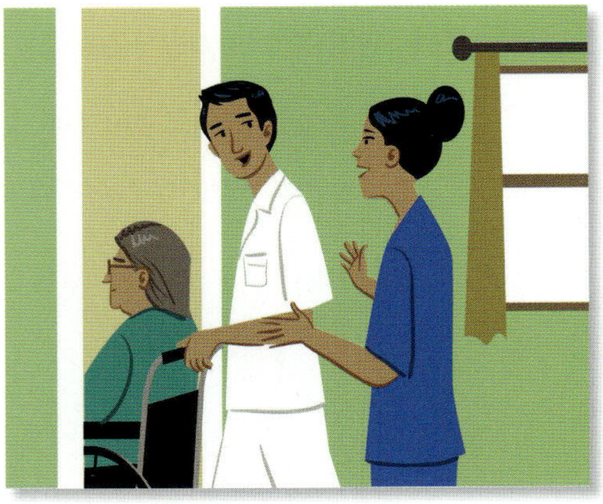

1 Before you read

Look at the picture. Answer the questions.

1. Who are these people?
2. What are they doing?

2 Read

Read the recommendation email. Listen and read again.

CD2, Track 19

New Message

Dear Mr. O'Hara:

I am happy to write this recommendation for Marco Alba. Marco started working at Valley Hospital as an orderly in 2016. He takes patients from their rooms to the lab, delivers X-rays, and takes flowers and mail to patients. He also delivers linens and supplies. He is an excellent worker, and his co-workers like him very much.

We are sorry to lose Marco. He wants to go to school and needs to work part-time, but we don't have a part-time job for him right now. I recommend Marco very highly. Please contact me for more information.

Suzanne Briggs
Human Resources Assistant
Valley Hospital

Look through the text quickly for specific information, like names and dates.
Marco Alba 2016

CULTURE NOTE
Teachers and employers often write recommendation letters or emails to help you get a job or get into a school.

3 After you read

Write. Answer the questions about the email. Write complete sentences.

1. When did Marco start his job at Valley Hospital? *He started his job in 2016.*
2. What does he do there? ______
3. Why is Marco leaving? ______
4. Who wrote the email? ______
5. Why did Suzanne write the email? ______
6. Which word in the email means *to make a positive comment*? ______
7. Mr. O'Hara has a question about Marco. Who should he ask? ______

4 Picture dictionary Job duties

1. repair cars

2. ______________

3. ______________

4. ______________

5. ______________

6. ______________

7. ______________

8. ______________

9. ______________

A **Write** the words in the Picture dictionary. Then listen and repeat.

assist the doctor	handle money	prepare food
assist the pharmacist	help the nurses	repair cars
clear tables	operate large machines	take care of a family

CD2, Track 20

B **Talk** with a partner. Match the pictures with the jobs.

a busperson	a cook	a pharmacy technician
a cashier	a homemaker	an auto technician
a construction worker	a medical assistant	an orderly

He repairs cars.

He's an auto mechanic.

For college and career readiness practice, see pages 150–151.

Identify the main idea and key details in a recommendation email; use vocabulary for job duties

Lesson E Writing

1 Before you write

A **Talk** with a partner. Ask and answer the questions.

1. What are some of your duties at home?
2. What are some of your duties at your job?
3. What were some of your duties at your last job?

B **Read** Marco's employment history. Complete the sentences. Use the correct form of the verb.

Capitalize the names of businesses: ***V**alley **H**ospital*

Employment History: Marco Alba

Marco Alba is an orderly. He *works* (1. work) at Valley Hospital. He started in 2017. He ______ (2. have) many duties. He ______ (3. take) patients from their rooms to the lab. He ______ (4. deliver) X-rays, linens, and supplies. He also ______ (5. take) flowers and mail to patients.

From 2015 to 2017, Marco ______ (6. work) at Sam's Soup and Sandwich Shop. He ______ (7. be) a busperson. He ______ (8. clean) the floor and ______ (9. pick up) dirty dishes. From 2012 to 2015, he ______ (10. work) at Fratelli's Construction Company. He ______ (11. be) a construction worker. He ______ (12. make) repairs on houses and ______ (13. operate) large machines.

C **Write** Marco's job duties now and in the past.

Now	In the past
1. *He takes patients from their rooms to the lab.*	1.
2.	2.
3.	3.
	4.

D **Write.** Answer the questions about yourself. Complete the side that is true about you.

Do you have a job? Yes?	Do you have a job? No?
Answer these questions.	Answer these questions.
1. What is your job? ____	1. Where do you study? ____
2. Where do you work? ____	2. What do you study at school? ____
3. What are your duties? ____	3. Did you have a job before? What jobs did you have? ____
4. Did you have a job before? What jobs did you have? ____	4. Where did you work? ____
5. Where did you work? ____	5. What were your duties? ____
6. What were your duties? ____	

2 Write

Write two paragraphs about your employment history. In the first paragraph, write about the present. In the second paragraph, write about the past. Use Exercises 1B and 1D to help you.

3 After you write

A **Read** your employment history to a partner.

B **Check** your partner's employment history.

- What are the jobs?
- What are the duties?
- Do the names of businesses start with capital letters?

Lesson F Another view

1 Life-skills reading

LARRY'S DISCOUNT STORE — WEEKLY TIME SHEET

Employee: *Lara da Silva*   Social Security Number: *000-99-0531*   Rate: *$14.00/hour*

DAY	DATE	TIME IN	TIME OUT	TIME IN	TIME OUT	HOURS
Monday	8/7	9:00 a.m.	12:00 noon	1:00 p.m.	4:00 p.m.	6
Tuesday	8/8	8:30 a.m.	12:30 p.m.	1:30 p.m.	5:30 p.m.	8
Wednesday	8/9	9:00 a.m.	2:00 p.m.	3:00 p.m.	7:00 p.m.	9
Thursday	8/10	7:30 a.m.	12:30 p.m.	1:30 p.m.	3:30 p.m.	7
Friday	8/11	9:00 a.m.	12:00 noon	1:00 p.m.	5:00 p.m.	7
TOTAL HOURS						37

I have worked these hours. I understand that false information will result in my termination with the company.

Employee's signature: *Lara da Silva*   Date: 8/14/17

Supervisor's signature: Helen Wilson   Date: 8/14/17

A **Read** the questions. Look at the time sheet. Fill in the answer.

1. What is Lara's hourly rate?
   - (A) 9:00–5:00
   - (B) 8 hours
   - (C) $14
   - (D) $37

2. When did Lara start work on Tuesday?
   - (A) 7:30 a.m.
   - (B) 8:30 a.m.
   - (C) 9:00 a.m.
   - (D) 9:30 a.m.

3. Which statement is true?
   - (A) Laura left work at 4:00 on Thursday.
   - (B) Laura started work at 12 on Tuesday.
   - (C) Laura started work at 8:30 on Tuesday.
   - (D) Laura worked for 8 hours on Friday.

4. What day did Lara start work at 7:30?
   - (A) Monday
   - (B) Tuesday
   - (C) Wednesday
   - (D) Thursday

B **Solve** the problem. Which solution is best? Circle your opinion.

Laura worked for 37 hours last week, but the company only paid her for 35 hours. What should she do?

1. Call the manager.
2. Wait until next month to see if the two hours are on the check.
3. Nothing.
4. Other: ______________________

2 Grammar connections: *could / couldn't* and *can / can't* (past and present ability)

Use *can* and *can't* to talk about ability to do something in the present.
Use *could* and *couldn't* to talk about ability to do something in the past.

PAST	PRESENT
I **could** dance as a child.	I **can** dance now.
I **could** run fast as a child.	I **can't** run fast now.
I **couldn't** type fast before.	I **can't** type fast now.

couldn't = could not
can't = cannot

Watch

A **Work with a partner.** Look at the pictures. Talk about your abilities before and now.

A I *couldn't* drive a car before, but I *can* drive a car now.
B I *could* drive a car before, and I *can* drive a car now.

USEFUL LANGUAGE
last year
as a child
two / five / ten years ago
a few years ago

1. drive

2. play the piano

3. take care of children

4. check email

5. read in English

6. cook

B **Work with your partner.** Ask and answer the questions.

1. What couldn't you do as a child that you can do now?
2. What could you do as a child that you can't do now?

REVIEW

1 Listening

Read the questions. Then listen and circle the answers.

CD2, Track 21

1. What does Yuri do?
   (a.) He's a salesperson.
   b. He's a manager.
2. Why did the Chans want a new sofa?
   a. Their sofa wasn't clean.
   b. Their sofa wasn't comfortable.
3. Which sofa was cheaper?
   a. the first sofa
   b. the second sofa
4. Why did they like the second sofa?
   a. It was bigger and more comfortable.
   b. It was nicer and more expensive.
5. What did Mr. and Mrs. Chan buy?
   a. a sofa and two lamps
   b. a sofa and an entertainment center
6. Where did Yuri go after work?
   a. to a supermarket
   b. to a restaurant

Talk with a partner. Ask and answer the questions. Use complete sentences.

2 Grammar

A **Write.** Complete the story.

VANESSA'S LAST JOB

Last year, Vanessa ___worked___ (1. work) the day shift at the Hometown Hotel. First, she __________ (2. go) to the supply room at 8:00 a.m. Next, she __________ (3. take) her cart to the third floor. Then, she __________ (4. make) the beds. After that, she __________ (5. clean) the rooms and __________ (6. pick up) dirty linens. Vanessa's job __________ (7. not / be) easy, but she liked it because she __________ (8. meet) a lot of nice people.

B **Write.** Look at the answers. Write the questions.

1. **A** Where ___did Vanessa work last year___?
   B Vanessa worked at the Hometown Hotel last year.
2. **A** What shift __________________?
   B She worked the day shift.
3. **A** When __________________?
   B She went to the supply room at 8:00 a.m.
4. **A** Where __________________?
   B She took her cart to the third floor.

Talk with a partner. Ask and answer the questions.

3 Pronunciation: the *-ed* ending in regular simple past verbs

A **Listen** to the *-ed* endings in these simple past verbs.

/d/	/t/	/ɪd/
us**ed** She used the new machine.	help**ed** He helped the nurses.	want**ed** They wanted to make the beds.
deliver**ed** You delivered the mail.	work**ed** He worked on the weekends.	assist**ed** She assisted the patient.

CD2, Track 22

B **Listen and repeat.**

/d/	/t/	/ɪd/
repaired	picked	needed
prepared	cooked	started
played	walked	visited

CD2, Track 23

C **Listen** and check (✓) the correct column.

	/d/	/t/	/ɪd/		/d/	/t/	/ɪd/
1. cleaned	✓			5. pushed			
2. operated				6. checked			
3. finished				7. answered			
4. handled				8. reported			

CD2, Track 24

D **Write** six regular verbs from Units 7 and 8 in the simple past. Check (✓) the correct column.

	/d/	/t/	/ɪd/		/d/	/t/	/ɪd/
1.				4.			
2.				5.			
3.				6.			

Talk with a partner. Make a sentence with each verb. Take turns.

UNIT 9 DAILY LIVING

Lesson A Listening

1 Before you listen

A Look at the picture. What do you see?

B Point to: ■ a dishwasher ■ a leak ■ a light bulb ■ a lock ■ a dryer ■ garbage ■ a sink ■ a washing machine

C Look at the woman. What's she doing?

2 Listen

A **Listen.** Who is Stella talking to? Write the letter of the conversation.

CD2, Track 25

1. ____

2. ____

3. ____

B **Listen again.** Write *T* (true) or *F* (false).

CD2, Track 25

Conversation A

1. Stella lives in Apartment 4B. T
2. Stella is talking to a plumber. ____
3. Don Brown is a neighbor. ____

Conversation B

4. Stella wants to speak to her husband. ____
5. Don Brown will come in one hour. ____
6. Stella will unlock the door for the plumber. ____

Conversation C

7. Russell wants Stella to call a neighbor. ____
8. Stella already called the plumber. ____
9. Stella is going to school. ____

Listen again. Check your answers. Correct the false statements.

3 After you listen

Talk with a partner. Ask and answer the questions.

1. Who fixes things in your home?
2. Did you ever need to call a plumber or other repair person?
3. Who did you call?
4. What happened?

Lesson B Can you call a plumber, please?

1 Grammar focus: requests with *Can*, *Could*, *Will*, or *Would*

Use *can, could, will,* or *would* before the base form of the verb to request help. Use short answers to say *yes* or *no* politely.

QUESTIONS			SHORT ANSWERS
Can	you	**call** a plumber, please?	Sure. I'd be happy to.
Could			Yes, of course.
Will			No, not now. Maybe later.
Would			Sorry, I can't right now.

Watch

2 Practice

A **Write.** Complete the conversations. Use *What* or *Where* and the simple past.

1. fix the dryer

2. unclog the sink

3. clean the carpet

4. repair the oven

5. fix the lock

6. fix the window

7. repair the dishwasher

8. change the light bulb

1. **A** Could *you fix the dryer, please*?
   B Yes, of course.
2. **A** Can ____________________?
   B No, not now. Maybe later.
3. **A** Would ____________________?
   B Sorry, I can't right now.
4. **A** Will ____________________?
   B Sure. I'd be happy to.
5. **A** Will ____________________?
   B No, not now. Maybe later.
6. **A** Could ____________________?
   B Yes, of course.
7. **A** Would ____________________
   B Sure. I'd be happy to.
8. **A** Can ____________________?
   B Sorry, I can't right now.

Listen and repeat. Then practice with a partner.

CD2, Track 26

B **Talk** with a partner. Change the **bold** words and make conversations.

A Can you **fix the window**, please?
B Yes, of course.

1. fix the window
2. repair the refrigerator
3. unclog the sink
4. fix the toilet
5. repair the oven

A Would you **fix the stove**, please?
B Sorry, I can't right now.

6. fix the front burner
7. fix the light
8. repair the cabinet drawer
9. repair the lock
10. fix the outlet

3 Communicate

Write. What are some problems in your home or in a friend's home? Make a list of requests for the landlord.

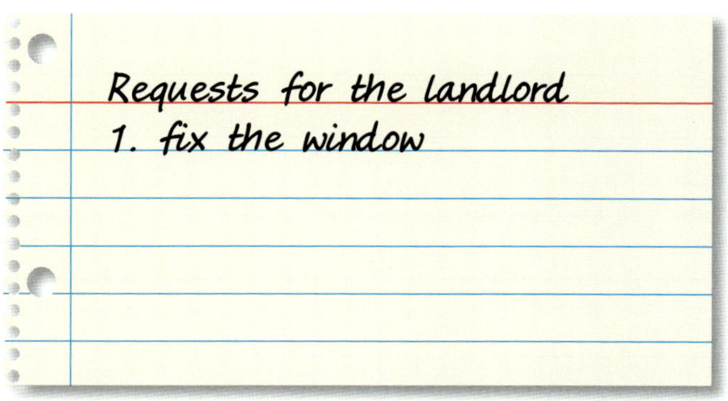

CULTURE NOTE
A *tenant* rents an apartment or house from the *landlord*. The landlord is the owner.

Talk. Role-play with a partner. One person is the tenant. The other is the landlord.

Tenant: Could you fix the window, please?
Landlord: Yes, of course. I'll be there tomorrow.

Lesson C Which one do you recommend?

1 Grammar focus: *Which* questions and simple present

Use *which* to ask a question about a choice between two or more items.

QUESTIONS					ANSWERS		
Which	plumbing service	**do**	you	**recommend**?	I	**recommend**	Purdy's Plumbing.
		does	he		He	**recommends**	
		do	they		They	**recommend**	

Watch

2 Practice

CULTURE NOTE
Plumbers and electricians are usually licensed. You can ask to see their license.

HARRISON'S Plumbing Service
Clean and Professional
555-8000

- $100 an hour
- Open 24 hours a day / 7 days a week
- Fast
- 30 years of experience

BROWN'S Plumbing Service

- Complete plumbing service
- $50 an hour
- Licensed
- 15 years of experience
- Insured

555-7407

A Write. Complete the conversations. Use **Which** and the simple present.

1. **A** (you / recommend) *Which plumbing service do you recommend – Harrison's or Brown's?*
   B (cheaper) *I recommend Brown's Plumbing Service because it's cheaper.*
2. **A** (he / recommend) __________
   B (fast) __________
3. **A** (they / recommend) __________
   B (licensed) __________
4. **A** (she / recommend) __________
   B (insured) __________
5. **A** (they / recommend) __________
   B (experienced) __________
6. **A** (he / recommend) __________
   B (open 24 hours a day) __________

Listen and repeat. Then practice with a partner.

CD2, Track 27

B **Talk** with a partner. Change the **bold** words and make conversations.

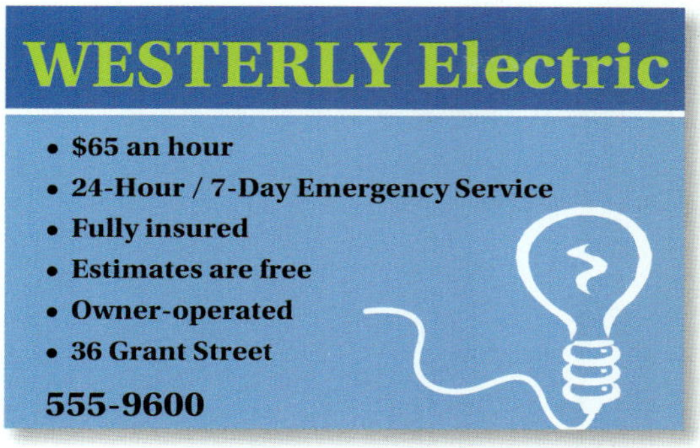

A Which electric service do you recommend?

B I recommend **Westerly Electric** because it's **open 24 hours a day**.

CULTURE NOTE
An *owner-operated* business is usually small and friendly.

1. open 24 hours a day
2. fully licensed
3. owner-operated
4. open 7 days a week
5. on Main Street
6. fully insured
7. cheaper
8. less expensive per hour

3 Communicate

For each place, write two or three names of businesses in your community.

1. supermarkets ______________________
2. restaurants ______________________
3. pharmacies ______________________
4. gas stations ______________________
5. banks ______________________
6. department stores ______________________
7. fast food restaurants ______________________
8. coffee shops ______________________

Talk with your classmates. Ask and answer questions about the places in your community.

Which supermarket do you like?

I like Acme Supermarket because it's cheap.

I prefer SaveMore Supermarket on Broadway because it's clean.

USEFUL LANGUAGE
I recommend . . .
I suggest . . .
I like . . .
I prefer . . .

Lesson D Reading

1 Before you read

Look at the picture. Answer the questions.

1. Who is the woman?
2. What's the problem?

2 Read

Read Stella's notice. Listen and read again.

CD2, Track 28

Attention, tenants:

Do you have problems in your apartment?
Is anyone fixing them?

- Many tenants have broken windows.
- Tenants on the third floor have no lights in the hall.
- A tenant on the second floor has a leaking ceiling.
- Tenants on the first floor smell garbage every day.

I'm really upset! We need to get together and write a letter of complaint to the manager of the building.

Come to a meeting Friday night at 7:00 p.m. in Apartment 4B.

Stella Taylor, Tenant 4B

Sometimes it is not necessary to know the exact meaning of a word. It is enough to know if the meaning is positive (good) or negative (not good).

upset, complaint = negative

3 After you read

Write. Answer the questions about Stella's notice.
Write complete sentences.

1. Which tenant has a leaking ceiling? *A tenant on the second floor has a leaking ceiling.*
2. Which tenants have no lights in the hall? ______
3. In the notice, what is another word for *unhappy*? ______
4. Why did Stella write this notice? ______
5. Where is the meeting? ______
6. Does the building manager do a good job? Why or why not?

______

4 Picture dictionary Home problems

1. *broken*

2. ____________

3. ____________

4. ____________

5. ____________

6. ____________

7. ____________

8. ____________

9. ____________

A **Write** the words in the Picture dictionary. Then listen and repeat.

bent	burned out	dripping	scratched	torn
broken	cracked	jammed	stained	

CD2, Track 29

B **Talk** with a partner. Change the bold words and make conversations.

A What's the problem?

B **My window is broken**. Could you fix it, please?

A Sure. I'll try.

For college and career readiness practice, see pages 152–153.

Identify the main idea and key details in a tenant notice: use vocabulary for home problems

Lesson E Writing

1 Before you write

A **Talk** in a group. Ask and answer the questions.

1. Did you ever have a problem in your apartment?
2. What was the problem?
3. Did you tell the landlord about the problem?
4. Did you write a letter or email to the landlord?

Emails usually have three parts:
1. the name of the person it is written to,
2. the subject of the email, and
3. the message.
Some people will not open an email without a subject.

B **Read** the letter of complaint.

New Message

to — **To:** Derek Betcher

subject — **Subject:** Apartment Problems

From: Stella Taylor <staylor@micro.com>

message —

I am a tenant at 3914 Fifth Street. I am writing to you about the many problems in the apartment building.

My neighbors and I made a list of problems in our apartments. The list of problems is in the attachment. Many things are broken, leaking, clogged or jammed, and we are very upset. Could you please send a repair person to fix these things immediately?

You can contact me at 713-555-1944 if you have additional questions. You can also come and talk to me. I live in Apartment 4B.

Thank you for your attention to these apartment problems.

Stella Taylor
Chairperson, Tenants Committee

C **Write.** Answer the questions about Stella's letter.

1. What is the subject of the email? *Apartment Problems*
2. Who is the email to? ______________________
3. What is Stella's title? ______________________
4. What is in the email attachment? ______________________
5. In the email, what is a word that means *quickly*? ______________________

D **Write.** Read the list of problems. Complete the sentences.

broken clogged cracked jammed leaking stained

Problems at 3914 Fifth Street

Apartment 1F
The carpet is ____________________ .
1

Apartment 2C
The front door lock is ____________________ .
2

Apartment 3A
The bedroom walls are ____________________ .
3

Apartment 4B
The living room window is ____________________ .
4

Apartment 5B
The refrigerator is ____________________ .
5

Apartment 6D
The kitchen sink is ____________________ .
6

2 Write

Write a complaint email to your building manager or landlord. Use Exercises 1B and 1D to help you.

3 After you write

A **Read** your email to a partner.

B **Check** your partner's email.

- What are the problems?
- Who is the email to?
- Does the email have a subject?

Lesson F Another view

1 Life-skills reading

A+ PLUMBING REPAIRS
Montague, New Jersey 07827
(973) 555-2399 • 30-day guarantee on all repairs

Customer Invoice 102051

CUSTOMER NAME *Victor Waters*
CUSTOMER ADDRESS *1872 Valley Street*
Newton, New Jersey 07860
SERVICE TECHNICIAN *Russ*
DATE *March 17, 2018*

DESCRIPTION		AMOUNT
SINK CLOGGED		$55.00
SHOWER LEAKING		$45.00
TOILET OVERFLOWED		$95.00
	SUBTOTAL	$195.00
	TAX	$13.65
	TOTAL	$208.65

A **Read** the questions. Look at the invoice. Fill in the answer.

1. What was leaking?
   - (A) the sink
   - (B) the shower
   - (C) the toilet
   - (D) the dishwasher

2. Which repair was the most expensive?
   - (A) the sink
   - (B) the shower
   - (C) the toilet
   - (D) the dishwasher

3. How much is the subtotal?
   - (A) $13.65
   - (B) $208.65
   - (C) $195.00
   - (D) $95.00

4. What is another word on the form for *bill*?
   - (A) invoice
   - (B) guarantee
   - (C) technician
   - (D) service

B **Solve** the problem. Which solution is best? Circle your opinion.

A+ Plumbing fixed Victor's bathroom shower on March 17. On March 31, the same shower leaked again. What should Victor do?

1. Call a new plumber. A+ did a bad job.
2. Fix the shower himself.
3. Call the same plumber. The work is guaranteed.
4. Other: ______________________

2 Grammar connections: *let's and let's not*

Use *let's* + base form of verb form of *let's not* + base form of verb to make suggestions.

Let's buy a new refrigerator.

Let's not fix the dishwasher.

let's = let us

Watch

A **Work with a group.** Look at the kitchen and the list. You have $2,000. What do you want to buy, change, or fix? Make suggestions.

A *Let's buy* a new refrigerator.

B Great. *Let's do* that.

C No, *let's not get* a new one. It's too expensive. *Let's repair* the old one.

2 cans of paint	$65
New table	$150
New chairs	$50 each
New refrigerator	$950
Refrigerator repair	$300
New stove	$599
Stove repair	$200
New dishwasher	$549
Dishwasher repair	$200
New sink	$400
Sink repair	$150
New window	$350
Light	$45 each
Light bulb	$5 each

B **Work with your group.** Think of ways to improve your classroom.

A Let's bring more books in English for people to read.

B Let's get some free magazines.

Scan an invoice for key details: use *let's* and *let's not* to make suggestions

UNIT 10 FREE TIME

Lesson A Listening

1 Before you listen

A Look at the picture. What do you see?

B Point to: ■ a graduation cake ■ flowers ■ a guest ■ perfume ■ a piece of cake ■ balloons ■ a present

C Look at the people. What are they doing?

2 Listen

A Listen. Which gift is Celia talking about? Write the letter of the conversation.

CD2, Track 30

1. ____

2. ____

3. ____

B Listen again. Write *T* (true) or *F* (false).

CD2, Track 30

Conversation A

1. Celia is having a birthday party. F
2. Celia's mother made a cake. ____
3. Aunt Ana would like some cake. ____

Conversation B

4. Mrs. Campbell is a student. ____
5. Celia started English class three years ago. ____
6. Mrs. Campbell brought Celia a card. ____

Conversation C

7. Sue brought her children to the party. ____
8. Sue would like some water. ____
9. Sue gave Celia some balloons. ____

Listen again. Check your answers. Correct the false statements.

3 After you listen

Talk with a partner. Ask and answer the questions.

1. Does your family celebrate graduations?
2. How does your family celebrate them?
3. What other special days does your family celebrate?

CULTURE NOTE
People often celebrate someone's graduation with a party for family and friends.

Lesson B Would you like some cake?

1 Grammar focus: *Would you like . . . ? What would you like?*

Use *Would you like* . . . to offer something to someone in the present or future.

QUESTIONS				ANSWERS		
Would	you / he / they	**like**	some cake?	Yes,	I / he / they	**would**.
				No, thank you.		

QUESTIONS				ANSWERS		
What	**would**	you / she / they	**like**?	I'**d** / She'**d** / They'**d**	**like**	some cake.

Watch

I'd = I would
He'd = He would
She'd = She would
They'd = They would

2 Practice

A **Write.** Complete the conversations. Use contractions to answer the *What* questions.

1. **A** ___Would you like___ (you) a cup of coffee?
   B Yes, ___I would___.
2. **A** ________________ (she) some ice cream?
   B Yes, ________________.
3. **A** ________________ (they) some salad?
   B Yes, ________________.
4. **A** ________________ (he) a hot dog?
   B No, ____________. He just ate one.
5. **A** ________________ (you) some cake?
   B No, ____________. I am not hungry.
6. **A** ___What would she like___ (she)?
   B ___She'd like___ a balloon.
7. **A** ________________ (you)?
   B ________________ a sandwich.
8. **A** ________________ (they)?
   B ________________ some tea.
9. **A** ________________ (he)?
   B ________________ some water.
10. **A** ________________ (she)?
    B ________________ rice and chicken.

Listen and repeat. Then practice with a partner.

CD2, Track 31

B **Talk** with a partner. Change the **bold** words and make conversations.

A What would **you** like?
B **I'd** like **some cake**, please.

1. you / some cake

2. they / some fruit

3. she / a piece of pie

4. they / some cheese

5. he / a bottle of water

6. you / some cookies

7. he / some soda

8. she / some dessert

9. you / a cup of tea

3 Communicate

Talk with a partner. Make conversations.

A Would you like something to drink?
B Yes, please.
A What would you like?
B I'd like some soda, please.
A Would you like something to eat?
B No, thank you. I'm full.

USEFUL LANGUAGE
Would you like something to drink?
Would you like something to eat?
Yes, please. / No, thank you. I'm full.

Lesson C Tim gave Mary a present.

1 Grammar focus: direct and indirect objects

A direct object answers the question *What?* (a present). An indirect object says *who receives* the direct object (Mary).

STATEMENTS

		Direct object		Indirect object
Tim	gave bought	**a present**	to for	**Mary.** **her.**

		Indirect object	Direct object
Tim	gave bought	**Mary** **her**	**a present.**

Irregular verbs
buy → bought
give → gave
send → sent
write → wrote

give + to = give **to** someone
buy + for = buy **for** someone

Watch

2 Practice

A Write. Look at Joe's "to do" list. What did he do yesterday? Write sentences.

To do
- ✔ *buy flowers for Sylvia*
- ✔ *buy a card for Nick*
- ✔ *write a letter to Pam*
- ✔ *buy a cake for Mary and Judy*
- ✔ *give roses to Eva*
- ✔ *send an invitation to Paul*
- ✔ *send some money to David*
- ✔ *give a ride to Sue*

1. *Joe bought flowers for Sylvia.*
2. ______
3. ______
4. ______
5. ______
6. ______
7. ______
8. ______

Write. Complete the conversations. Use a pronoun for the indirect object.

1. **A** What did Joe buy Sylvia?
   B *Joe bought her flowers.*
2. **A** What did Joe buy Nick?
   B ______
3. **A** What did Joe write Pam?
   B ______
4. **A** What did Joe buy Mary and Judy?
   B ______
5. **A** What did Joe give Eva?
   B ______
6. **A** What did Joe send Paul?
   B ______
7. **A** What did Joe send David?
   B ______
8. **A** What did Joe give Sue?
   B ______

Listen and repeat. Then practice with a partner.

CD2, Track 32

B **Talk** with a partner. Change the **bold** words and make conversations.

A What did **Maria** give **Daniel**?
B She gave **him some balloons**.
A That's nice.

USEFUL LANGUAGE
I → *me*
he → *him*
she → *her*
they → *them*

1. some balloons

2. a card

3. some flowers

4. some cookies

5. some perfume

6. some books

7. some money

8. a gift certificate

3 Communicate

Write. Choose three classmates. Choose three items from your desk. Give one thing to each classmate. Then complete the chart.

Classmates	Items
Anika	*my Ventures book*
1.	
2.	
3.	

Talk with a partner. Share your information.

I gave Anika my *Ventures* book.

I gave Rudy my pen.

Ask for your things back.

Anika, please give me my *Ventures* book.

Rudy, please give me my pen.

Lesson D Reading

1 Before you read

Look at the picture. Answer the questions.

1. Who is the woman?
2. What is she doing?

2 Read

Read Stella's post. Listen and read again.

CD2, Track 33

Celia

I had a graduation party last Friday. My husband sent invitations to my teacher and to my relatives and friends. They all came to the party! My teacher, Mrs. Campbell, gave me a card. Some guests brought gifts for me. My Aunt Ana brought me flowers. My friend Sue gave me some perfume. My classmate, Ruth, brought me some cookies. After the party, I wrote them thank-you notes. Tomorrow, I'm going to mail the thank-you notes at the post office.

Celia Your status #hashtag

Look for examples of the main idea when you read. This paragraph is about gifts. Look for examples of all the gifts.

3 After you read

Write. Answer the questions about Celia's graduation party. Write complete sentences.

1. Who came to the party? *Celia's teacher, relatives, and friends came to the party.*
2. Which sentence in the paragraph states the main idea? ______
3. How many gifts did Celia receive? ______
4. What did Sue give Celia? ______
5. Who is an example of a "relative" in the paragraph? ______
6. What did Celia do after the party? ______
7. What is Celia going to do tomorrow? ______

4 Picture dictionary Celebrations

1. Thanksgiving 2. ____ 3. ____

4. ____ 5. ____ 6. ____

7. ____ 8. ____ 9. ____

A **Write** the words in the Picture dictionary. Then listen and repeat.

a baby shower	Halloween	New Year's Eve
a housewarming	Independence Day	Thanksgiving
a wedding	Mother's Day	Valentine's Day

CD2, Track 34

B **Talk** with a partner. What special days do you celebrate? How do you celebrate them?

Do you celebrate Thanksgiving?

Yes, we do. We always go to my mother-in-law's house for a big turkey dinner.

For college and career readiness practice, see pages 154–155.

Identify the main idea and key details in a paragraph about a graduation party; use vocabulary for celebrations

Lesson E Writing

1 Before you write

A **Talk** with a partner. Ask and answer the questions.

1. Did you ever receive a thank-you note?
2. Did you ever send someone a thank-you note?
3. In other countries, when do people write thank-you notes?

Indent the paragraphs in an informal note. Place the date on the right side. Don't indent *Dear*____.

B **Read** the thank-you note.

June 30, 2018

Dear Aunt Ana,

Thank you for the lovely flowers you gave me for my graduation. They are beautiful! I really like the color of the roses. Red is my favorite color!

Thank you so much for coming to my graduation party. I hope you had a good time.

Love,
Celia

CULTURE NOTE
It is polite to thank someone for a gift. A thank you note identifies the gift and says something about why you like it. People often write notes by hand, but you can also email or text or call someone to thank them.

C **Write.** Answer the questions about Celia's note. Write complete sentences.

1. When did Celia write the note?
   Celia wrote the note on June 30, 2018.
2. Who did Celia write the note to?
   ____
3. What did Aunt Ana give Celia?
   ____
4. Why did Celia like the gift?
   ____

D **Write.** Complete the thank-you note.

Best wishes	color	fun	shirt
birthday	Dear	party	size

_______________ (today's date)

_______________ (1) John,

Thank you for the beautiful _______________ (2) you gave me for my _______________ (3). It is just the right _______________ (4). I also really like the _______________ (5).

Thank you so much for coming to my _______________ (6). I hope you had _______________ (7).

_______________ (8),

Paula

CULTURE NOTE
Use *Love* or *Best wishes* in a personal note. Use *Sincerely* in a formal letter.

E **Write.** Answer the questions.

1. When did a friend give you a present? _______________
2. What is your friend's name? _______________
3. What was the present? _______________
4. Why did you like the present? _______________
5. What was the celebration? _______________

2 Write

Write a thank-you note to a friend for a gift. Use Exercises 1B, 1D, and 1E to help you.

3 After you write

A **Read** your note to a partner.

B **Check** your partner's note.

- What was the present?
- What was the celebration?
- Did your partner indent each paragraph?

Lesson F Another view

1 Life-skills reading

From: Tom_luisa
To: Will_katya
Subject: New Year's Eve Party

For: A New Year's Eve Party
Date: Wednesday, December 31
For: 8:00 p.m. until 1:00 a.m.
Place: Tom and Luisa's
76 North Street, Apt. 6A
RSVP: (813) 555-1234 by December 15

Please bring something to drink.
No children, please! Hope you can come!

A **Read** the questions. Look at the invitation. Fill in the answer.

1. What time will the party begin?
   - (A) 8:00 a.m.
   - (B) 1:00 p.m.
   - (C) 8:00 p.m.
   - (D) 1:00 a.m.
2. What does *RSVP* mean?
   - (A) Bring something to drink to the party.
   - (B) Reply to say 'yes' or 'no' to the invitation.
   - (C) Bring something to eat to the party.
   - (D) Send a thank-you note.
3. What should people bring to the party?
   - (A) something to drink
   - (B) something to eat
   - (C) their children
   - (D) nothing
4. Which statement is true?
   - (A) Tom and Luisa are giving the party.
   - (B) Will and Katya are giving the party.
   - (C) The party is from 8:00 p.m. to midnight.
   - (D) You need to reply after December 15.

B **Solve** the problem. Which solution is best? Circle your opinion.

Jose got an invitation to go to his friend's wedding. The invitation was addressed to Mr. and Mrs. Lopez. They have 3 children. What should he do?

1. Go to the wedding with his wife and 3 children.
2. Go to the wedding without his children.
3. Ask his friend if the children can go to the wedding.
4. Other: ____________________

2 Grammar connections: *there is / there are* and *there was / there were*

Use *there is / there are* to say that something exists in present time. Use *there was / there were* to say that something existed in the past.

PRESENT	PAST
There is a small cake on the table. **There isn't** any ice cream on the table.	**There was** a big cake on the table. **There wasn't** any fruit on the table.
There are four people at the party. **There aren't** any presents on the table.	**There were** six children at the party. **There weren't** any cards on the table.

Watch

A **Work with a partner.** Look at the pictures. Identify the differences. How many are there?

B **Work with your partner.** Talk about each difference. Take turns.

A The cakes are different. There's a small cake on the table today.
B There wasn't a small cake in 1985. There was a big birthday cake.

REVIEW

1 Listening

Read the questions. Then listen and circle the answers.

CD2, Track 35

1. Why is Ramona going to have a party?
   a. to celebrate her birthday
   (b.) to celebrate her new apartment
2. When is Ramona's party?
   a. next month
   b. next week
3. What does Ramona want to do?
   a. get her apartment ready
   b. fix the windows
4. How many good painters does Fabio know?
   a. one
   b. two
5. What is the name of the first painter?
   a. Fabio
   b. Walter
6. Which painter does Fabio recommend?
   a. the first one
   b. the second one

Talk with a partner. Ask and answer the questions. Use complete sentences.

2 Grammar

A **Write.** Complete the conversation.

Rita: Saba, could you *help* (1. help / helping) me with something? My teacher is going to retire tomorrow, and I want to buy a gift ______ (2. to / for) her. What should I get?

Saba: Would she ______ (3. like / likes) some flowers?

Rita: Yes, she ______ (4. will / would). She loves flowers. Where can I buy them?

Saba: There's a small flower shop downtown, and a bigger one near the school.

Rita: ______ (5. Which / Where) shop do you recommend?

Saba: I ______ (6. like / likes) the one near the school. It's cheaper.

B **Write.** Look at the answers. Write the questions.

1. **A** What *does Rita want to buy for her teacher*?
   B Rita wants to buy her teacher a gift.
2. **A** What ______?
   B Her teacher would like some flowers.
3. **A** Which ______?
   B Saba recommends the flower shop near the school.

Talk with a partner. Ask and answer the questions.

3 Pronunciation: the -s ending in the simple present

A **Listen** to the **-s** ending in these simple present verbs.

CD2, Track 36

/s/	/z/	/ɪz/
talks	is	watches
makes	has	fixes

B **Listen and repeat.**

CD2, Track 37

/s/	/z/	/ɪz/
wants	prefers	relaxes
suggests	recommends	teaches
unlocks	does	scratches

C **Listen** and check (✓) the correct column.

CD2, Track 38

Verb	/s/	/z/	/ɪz/	Verb	/s/	/z/	/ɪz/
1. drives				5. takes			
2. gets				6. wishes			
3. goes				7. sleeps			
4. uses				8. needs			

D **Write** six more verbs with **-s** endings in the simple present. Check (✓) the correct column for the pronunciation of the **-s** ending.

Verb	/s/	/z/	/ɪz/	Verb	/s/	/z/	/ɪz/
1.				4.			
2.				5.			
3.				6.			

Talk with a partner. Make a sentence with each word. Take turns.

Reading Tip: A photo can give important information. Look at the photo that goes with this e-invitation. What does the photo tell you about the e-invitation?

Sept
5

Teen Hike

Invitation from Morristown Teen Hikers Group

✓ Going ? Maybe × Can't Go … More

Saturday, September 5, 11:00-3:00

Meet at the soccer field in Washington Park

Are you 16-19 years old? Do you live in the Morristown area?

Join other teenagers on a hike to the Wakamori Japanese Garden.

- Meet between 10:30 and 11:00.
- Wear long pants, comfortable shoes, a long-sleeved shirt, a light jacket and a big hat.
- Bring a bag lunch, plenty of water and a couple of dollars for the Japanese Garden entrance fee.

1 Check your understanding

1. What is the purpose of this e-invitation?
2. What should people wear?
3. What should people bring?
4. Do you think this is a difficult hike? Why or why not?

2 Build your vocabulary

A Look at the phrases in Column 1. Then find the antonyms (words with opposite meanings) in the e-invitation. Underline them. Then write the antonyms in Column 2.

Phrase	Antonym in e-invitation
1. short pants	long pants
2. uncomfortable shoes	____________ shoes
3. heavy jacket	____________ jacket
4. small hat	____________ hat

B Find the academic words in Column 1 in the e-invitation and underline them. Then complete the chart.

Academic word	Phrase or sentence from e-invitation	Part of speech	Dictionary definition	My sentence
1. area	the Morristown area	noun	region	She is not from this area.
2. couple		noun		
3. fee		noun		

3 Talk with a partner

Answer each question with evidence from the e-invitation. Use the phrase in the Useful Language box.

1. How long is the teen hike?
2. Where is the group meeting?
3. Why do people need to bring money?

USEFUL LANGUAGE
According to the invitation, . . .

4 Analyze the texts

Objective: Compare two texts on the same topic.

Review the following texts to answer the questions below: (1) Student Book, p. 12, *Shoko's email* and (2) Extended reading, *Teen Hike*.

1. What is the topic of both?
2. What is one way they are similar?
3. What is one way they are different?

Reading Tip: A form is a printed paper with empty spaces to fill in. Forms often have words in bold. Bold words identify information to fill in. Look at the bold words. What information is the form asking for?

Student Self-Assessment

Name: *Joseph LeFavor*

MY GOAL: *Speak well in English with people outside class.*

What will you do? *I will find one or two native speakers to talk to.*
I will talk to them outside class.
I will do this 2 or 3 times a week.

My Progress

1. English is easier for me now because *I can participate in class and speak more English with my teacher and other students.*
2. English is still difficult for me because *speakers use vocabulary words I don't know. They also speak too fast and there are many different accents.*

My Results and Next Steps

1. Did you achieve your goal? *No. My English is better, but I haven't achieved my goal.*
   If yes, why? If no, why not? *I am afraid to make mistakes in English.*
2. What do you plan to do next? *I will continue trying to reach my goal.*
   I will talk to more than one or two native speakers.
   I will do this more than 2 or 3 times a week.

1 Check your understanding

1. What is the topic of this form?
2. What is Joseph's goal?
3. Did Joseph achieve his goal? What did he say?
4. Reread Joseph's answer. Why didn't he achieve his goal? Do you have the same problem?

2 Build your vocabulary

A Find the words in Column 1 on the Student Self-Assessment form. Underline them. Then, circle the definitions that best match the meaning of the words on the form.

Word on form	Definition that matches meaning on form
1. outside	(a.) interior b. exterior
2. reach	a. not finish, give up b. attain, achieve
3. mistakes	a. something wrong b. something right
4. plan	a. decide how to do something b. do things without thinking about them first

B Find the academic words in Column 1 on the Student Self-Assessment form and underline them. Then complete the chart.

Academic word	Phrase or sentence from form	Part of speech	Dictionary definition	My sentence
1. achieve	*Did you achieve your goal?*	verb	*To reach, to gain*	*I achieved my goal.*
2. goal		noun		
3. participate		verb		

3 Talk with a partner

Answer each question with evidence from the form. Use the phrase in the Useful Language box.

1. What is easier for Joseph to do now?
2. What is still difficult for Joseph to do?
3. Why didn't Joseph reach his goal?

USEFUL LANGUAGE
According to the form, . . .

4 Analyze the texts

Objective: Compare two texts on the same topic.

Review the following texts to answer the questions below: (1) Student Book, p. 24, Joseph's application and (2) Extended reading, *Student Self-Assessment*.

1. What is the topic of both?
2. What is one way they are similar?
3. What is one way they are different?

Reading Tip: Tip sheets provide advice. Each tip begins with a bullet (•) or a number. They are written in a list. Look at the Tip Sheet. How many tips are there?

Reply Forward

From: Jorge Mendoza <jm@yournmail.com>
To: Rosa Mendoza <cambridge.org>
Subject: car breakdown

Dearest Rosa,

I'm so sorry you had a bad day yesterday. I want to be sure you are safe. I found this sheet. It provides tips. Keep it in the car.

Your loving husband

Tip Sheet

Your car breaks down – What should you do?

Remove your car from danger.

- Steer – don't push – the car to the far right shoulder of the road.

Keep the driver and passengers safe.

- Leave your vehicle. Don't stay in the car.
- Don't stand behind or in front of a disabled car.

Warn other drivers about your disabled car.

- Turn on the emergency lights to alert other drivers.
- Raise the car's hood.
- Light flares if you have them.

Finally, call a roadside service for assistance. Many of them have a fast response.

3 Check your understanding

1. What is the purpose of the email?
2. Your car breaks down. What are three things should you?
3. What should you do first?
4. Which tip for warning other drivers would you use? Why?

2 Build your vocabulary

A Find the words in Column 1 in the email and tip sheet. Underline them. Then circle the definition that best matches the meaning in the reading.

Word in reading	Definition that matches meaning in reading
1. provides	a. takes b. gives
2. disabled	a. broken b. fixed
3. alert	a. not noticing things b. noticing things
4. flares	a. lights b. signs

B Find the academic words in Column 1 in the email and tip sheet and underline them. Then complete the chart.

Academic word	Phrase or sentence from form	Part of speech	Dictionary definition	My sentence
1. assistance	*roadside service for assistance*	noun	*help*	*I need some assistance to move my furniture.*
2. remove		verb		
3. response		noun		

3 Talk with a partner

Answer each question with evidence from the tip sheet. Use the phrase in the Useful Language box.

1. Where should you steer your car?
2. How can you warn other drivers?
3. Should you stay in the car?

USEFUL LANGUAGE
According to the tip sheet, . . .

4 Analyze the texts

Objective: Compare two texts on the same topic.

Review the following texts to answer the questions below: (1) Student Book, p. 38, *Rosa's Journal*, and (2) Extended reading, *Your car breaks down – What should you do?*

1. What is the topic of both readings?
2. What is one way they are similar?
3. What is one way they are different?

UNIT 4

College and Career Readiness

Reading Tip: Each bulleted item (•) on a list is a key (or *important*) idea. Look at the warning. How many key ideas are there?

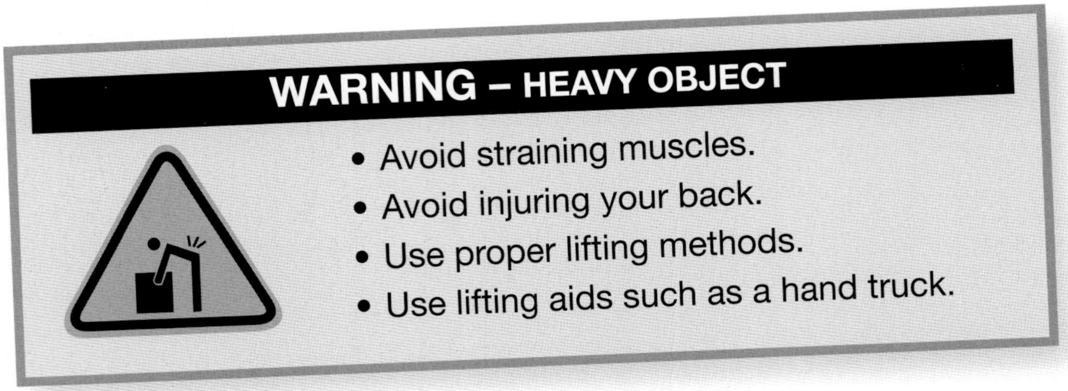

John's Problem

John works for a moving company. Every day, he first removes furniture from residences and businesses. Then, he loads the furniture onto a company truck. Finally, he unloads the furniture at the new home or business. He lifts many heavy things. But John has a problem. Yesterday he saw the doctor. The doctor said, "You have back injury. You must not lift anything. You should stay home. You shouldn't work. Your back requires rest."

1 Check your understanding

1. What is the main idea of the warning label?
2. What does it say to avoid?
3. What does it say to use?
4. Read the paragraph about John. Do you think he read the warning label? Why or why not?

2 Build your vocabulary

A Find in the words in Column 1 on the warning label and underline them. Then, circle the definitions that best match the meaning on the warning label.

Word on warning label	Definition that matches meaning on warning label
1. straining	a. hurting b. exercising
2. avoid	a. stay away from b. allow
3. proper	a. right b. wrong
4. aids	a. things that do not help b. equipment that helps

B Find the academic words in Column 1 on the warning label and in the story about John and underline them. Then complete the chart.

Academic word	Phrase or sentence from form	Part of speech	Dictionary definition	My sentence
1. injury	*You have a back injury.*	noun	*a hurt*	*She has an injury, but she won't go to the doctor.*
2. methods		verb		
3. requires		verb		

3 Talk with a partner

Answer each question with evidence from the story about John. Use the phrase in the Useful Language box.

1. Who does John work for?
2. What does he do?
3. What happened yesterday?

USEFUL LANGUAGE
According to the story, . . .

4 Analyze the texts

Objective: Compare two texts on the same topic.

Review the following texts to answer the questions below: (1) p. 50, the warning label and (2) p. 142, *John's Problem*.

1. What is the topic of both?
2. What is one way they are similar?
3. What is one way they are different?

Reading Tip: Bar graphs usually have important information on the left side and at the bottom. Look at the graph below. On the left side of the graph, you see popular places for summer vacations. What does the bottom of the graph show?

Bar graphs provide data (information and numbers) from research. The data helps us compare things. This bar graph gives data on popular destinations for summer holidays in the U.S. The source of this data is Statista. They do research for private and governmental agencies.

Popular places for summer vacations

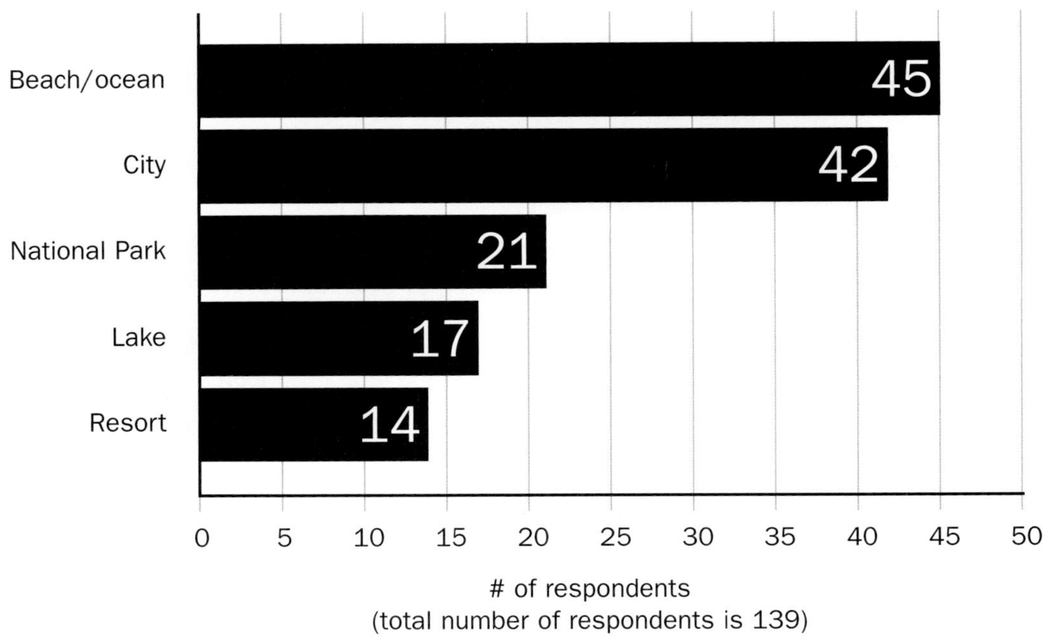

Source: Statista.com

1 Check your understanding

1. What is the main idea of the graph?
2. How many people responded to the question about popular summer vacation places?
3. What are the two most popular summer vacation destinations?
4. Read the graph again. Not many people go to resorts. What do you think is the reason?

2 Build your vocabulary

A An author often will use different words that have similar meanings. Find the words from Column 1 in the reading. Underline them. Then look at the reading again to find the words that have similar meanings. Circle them. Write the new words in Column 2 below.

Word in reading	Similar word in reading
1. beach	*ocean*
2. destination	
3. provide	
4. vacation	

B Find the academic words in Column 1 in the reading and underline them. Then complete the chart.

Academic word	Phrase or sentence from reading	Part of speech	Dictionary definition	My sentence
1. data	*Bar graphs provide data (information and numbers)*	noun	*facts about something that can be used in calculating and planning*	*I need data about high schools in this city.*
2. research		noun		
3. source		noun		

3 Talk with a partner

Answer each question with evidence from the graph. Use the phrase in the Useful Language box.

1. How many people enjoy going to lakes in the summer?
2. Which destination do people enjoy more—going to lakes or resorts?
3. How many people chose national parks as their favorite summer vacation destination?

USEFUL LANGUAGE
According to the graph, . . .

4 Analyze the texts

Objective: Compare two texts on the same topic.

Review the following texts to answer the questions below: (1) Student Book, p. 64, *Letter to Layla* and (2) Extended reading, *Popular places for summer vacations*.

1. What is the topic of both?
2. What is one way they are similar?
3. What is one way they are different?

Reading Tip: Dashes (-) often signal a definition, explanation, or example. Find the dash in Eduardo's story. Which does it signal – a definition, an explanation, or an example?

Spotlight on Eduardo Flores

Accounting Department Employee and New Father

My name is Eduardo Flores. I grew up with my grandparents in the Philippines. My parents came to the United States to find work and support the family. They worked very hard. Ten years ago, I decided to come to the United States to take care of them. It is a good thing I came. My mother died my first year here, and my father died a year later. It was very difficult to stay in the United States without my family. I was very lonely. I went to a local community college to study accounting and earned an accounting certificate. Then I got a job here. This large company has many employees. I especially liked one worker, a colleague in the accounting department. She was very capable and helped me when I had problems. Eventually, we started dating. After two years, I asked her to marry me and she said YES! Now we have twin boys – I'm not lonely anymore!

1 Check your understanding

1. What is the topic of the article?
2. Why did he come to this country?
3. Where did Eduardo go to college?
4. Do you think Eduardo is glad he came to this country? Why or why not?

2 Build your vocabulary

A Find the words in Column 1 in the article and underline them. Then write the phrase from the article in Column 2. After that, identify clues to meaning.

Word in article	Phrase from article	Clue to meaning
1. support	3. *large*	*find work*
2. lonely		
3. large		
3. large		

B Find the academic words in Column 1 in the article and underline them. Then complete the chart.

Academic word	Phrase or sentence from article	Part of speech	Dictionary definition	My sentence
1. capable	*She was very capable*	adjective	*skilled*	*They promoted him because he was capable.*
2. colleague		noun		
3. eventually		adverb		

3 Talk with a partner

Answer each question with evidence from the article. Use the phrase in the Useful Language box.

1. Why did Eduardo leave the Philippines?
2. How did Eduardo feel after his parents died?
3. How did he feel after he got married and had children?

USEFUL LANGUAGE
According to the article, . . .

4 Analyze the texts

Objective: Compare two texts on the same topic.

Review the following texts to answer the questions below: (1) Student Book, p. 76, *An Interesting Life*, and (2) Extended reading, *Spotlight on Eduardo Flores*.

1. What is the topic of both?
2. What is one way they are similar?
3. What is one way they are different?

UNIT 7

College and Career Readiness

Reading Tip: A photo can help you understand a reading. Look at the photo. What do you see? What can you say about the car?

80%

Used vehicles for sale, Chicago region

2004 Jeep Grand Cherokee, Spotless

Description

Seats six. Runs good. Spotless inside and out. Very well maintained.

Year: 2004	Make: Jeep	Model: Grand Cherokee
Mileage: 152,000	Condition: Excellent	Price: $4700 or best offer

Contact

Call or text (312) 555-8090 Or email: joe.baxter@cambridge.org

1 Check your understanding

1. What is the Internet ad about?
2. How much is the vehicle?
3. You want to buy this car. What should you do?
4. Do you think the price is good? Why or why not?

2 Build your vocabulary

A Find the words in Column 1 in the Internet ad and underline them. Then, circle the definitions that best match the meaning of the words in the Internet ad.

Word in Internet ad	Definition that matches meaning in the ad
1. make	(a.) kind of car b. color of car
2. mileage	a. cost per mile b. how many miles
3. excellent	a. very good b. very bad
4. spotless	a. no dirty spots b. many dirty spots

B Find the academic words in Column 1 in the Internet ad and underline them. Then complete the chart.

Academic word	Phrase or sentence from Internet ad	Part of speech	Dictionary definition	My sentence
1. region	*Chicago region*	noun	*area*	*This region of the country is cold in the winter.*
2. vehicles		noun		
3. well-maintained		adjective		

3 Talk with a partner

Answer each question with evidence from the Internet ad. Use the phrase in the Useful Language box.

1. How old is the vehicle?
2. Is the car clean or dirty?
3. How many people can sit in the car?

USEFUL LANGUAGE
According to the Internet ad, . . .

4 Analyze the texts

Objective: Compare two texts on the same topic.

Review the following texts to answer the questions below: (1) p. 90, *Today's Question*, and (2) p. 148, *Used Vehicles for Sale*.

1. What is the topic of both?
2. What is one way they are similar?
3. What is one way they are different?

Reading Tip: Important information is sometimes in bold. Look at the bold words in the Employee Evaluation. What information do the words in bold ask for?

Employee Evaluation

Date: April 20, 2017

Employee name: Jenni Espinoza

Job title: Sales Associate

Job duties: assist customers, keep fitting rooms clean and neat, work with team members

FT / PT (fill in): ○ PT ● FT

To the Evaluator: *For the evaluation, write one paragraph. Identify both strengths and weaknesses of the employee.*

Evaluation:

Jenni Espinoza is punctual and has a neat appearance. Her uniform is always clean and ironed. She is friendly and helpful to customers. She always asks, "Can I help you?" She follows the correct procedures with customers. For example, when a customer has a lot of questions, she answers them all and doesn't get impatient. She needs to check the fitting rooms more often. Sometimes they are messy or dirty. Jenni is an excellent part of our team and we hope one day she will be an assistant manager.

Evaluator's Signature: John Prince

1 Check your understanding

1. What is the main idea of the employee evaluation?
2. What two things does it say about Jenni's communication with customers?
3. Did the evaluator have suggestions for Jenni? What did he say?
4. Read the evaluation again. Do you think Jenni is a good sales associate? Why or why not?

2 Build your vocabulary

A Find the words in Column 1 in the employee evaluation and underline them. Does each word have a positive or negative meaning? Check the box. Finally, write the clues that helped you guess.

Word in employee evaluation	Positive	Negative	Clue that helped you decide
1. neat	☑	☐	*Her uniform is always clean and ironed.*
2. helpful	☐	☐	
3. messy	☐	☐	
4. excellent	☐	☐	

B Find the academic words in Column 1 in the employee evaluation and underline them. Then complete the chart.

Academic word	Phrase or sentence from evaluation	Part of speech	Dictionary definition	My sentence
1. evaluation	*For the evaluation, write one paragraph.*	noun	*A judgment about the amount, number or value of something*	*My evaluation at work was excellent.*
2. procedures		noun		
3. team		noun		

3 Talk with a partner

Answer each question with evidence from the employee evaluation. Use the phrase in the Useful Language box.

1. How does Jenni look at work?
2. What are the company's procedures on customer questions?
3. Why does Jenni need to check the fitting rooms more often?

USEFUL LANGUAGE
According to the evaluation, . . .

4 Analyze the texts

Objective: Compare two texts on the same topic.

Review the following texts to answer the questions below: (1) p. 102, the recommendation email and (2) p. 150, *Employee Evaluation.*

1. What is the topic of both?
2. What is one way they are similar?
3. What is one way they are different?

Reading Tip: Read the title of the article. Then read the headings of each column in the chart. Who made the complaints in Column 1? Who made the complaints in Column 2?

Common Complaints of Tenants and Managers

Tenants have many complaints about apartment managers. Apartment managers also have complaints. This chart identifies the four most common complaints from tenants and managers.

Tenants	Managers
• Managers don't make repairs.	• Tenants don't take care of apartments.
• Other tenants make too much noise.	• Tenants don't pay rent on time.
• Managers don't eliminate pests.	• Tenants allow other people to live in the apartment without permission.
• Managers don't refund security deposits when tenants move out.	• Tenants move out without paying the final month's rent.

1 Check your understanding

1. What is the topic?
2. What are two complaints that managers have?
3. What are two complaints that tenants have?
4. What do you think is the most common tenant complaint? Explain why. What do you think is the most common manager complaint? Explain why.

2 Build your vocabulary

A Find the words in Column 1 in the article and underline them. Then, circle the definitions that best match the meaning of the words in the article. Finally, use a dictionary or a thesaurus to find a synonym for each word.

Word in article	Meaning of word as used in article	Synonym
1. common	(a.) typical b. simple	*usual*
2. complaints	a. statements of unhappiness b. ailments	
3. pests	a. annoying people b. bugs, rats, mice	
4. refund	a. give a discount b. return money	

B Find the academic words in Column 1 in the article and underline them. Then complete the chart.

Academic word	Phrase or sentence from article	Part of speech	Dictionary definition	My sentence
1. chart	*This chart identifies the four most common complaints*	noun	*diagram or table*	*I can read the chart.*
2. eliminate		verb		
3. security		adjective		

3 Talk with a partner

Answer each question with evidence from the article. Use the phrase in the Useful Language box.

1. What do tenants say about repairs?
2. What do managers say about rent payments?
2. What do tenants say about security deposits?

USEFUL LANGUAGE
According to the chart, . . .

4 Analyze the texts

Objective: Compare two texts on the same topic.

Review the following texts to answer the questions below: (1) p. 116, *Attention tenants!*, and (2) p. 152, *Common Complaints of Tenants and Managers*.

1. What is the topic of both?
2. What is one way they are similar?
3. What is one way they are different?

Reading Tip: Bar graphs provide data and numbers from research. The data helps us compare things. Look at the left side of this graph. What does the graph compare? Look at the bottom of the graph. What does it tell you about each item on the left side of the graph?

Graduation Gift Survey

Businesses often contract with researchers to conduct surveys. The surveys ask questions, and the answers provide businesses with information. The graph below shows the results of a survey. The survey asked adults over 18 this question: "What type of item do you intend to purchase as a gift for a graduation?" Almost 7,200 adults in the United States answered. The graph below shows the results.

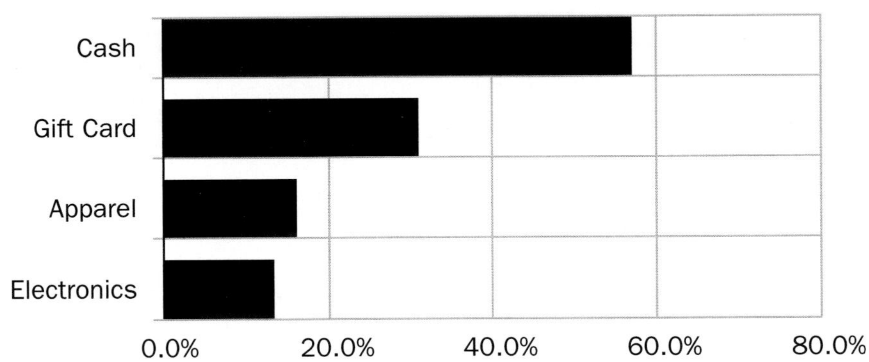

3 Check your understanding

1. What is the purpose of the graph?
2. What percent of adults over 18 years old plan to give a gift card as a graduation gift? About how many people is that?
3. According to the graph, what kind of gift is more popular – clothing or electronics?
4. Are the graduation gifts in the survey ones you give? If yes, which? If not, what do you give?

2 Build your vocabulary

A Find the words in Column 1 in the article and underline them. Then, circle the definitions that best match the meanings of the words in the article.

Word	Definition that matches meaning in article
1. intend	a. refuse (b.) plan
2. item	a. thing b. person
3. apparel	a. money b. clothes
4. type	a. kind b. write

B Find the academic words in Column 1 in the article and underline them. Then complete the chart.

Academic word	Phrase or sentence from article	Part of speech	Dictionary definition	My sentence
1. conduct	*conduct surveys*	verb	*To manage*	*He conducts business at that company.*
2. contract		verb		
3. survey		noun		

3 Talk with a partner

Answer each question with evidence from the article. Use the phrase in the Useful Language box.

1. What percent of adults 18 years and older will give cash for a graduation gift?
2. How many adults answered the survey?
3. What is the most popular gift?

USEFUL LANGUAGE
According to the survey, . . .

4 Analyze the texts

Objective: Compare two texts on the same topic.

Review the following texts to answer the questions below: (1) p. 128, Celia's post and (2) p. 154, *Graduation Gift Survey*.

1. What is the topic of both readings?
2. What is one way they are similar?
3. What is one way they are different?

AUDIO SCRIPT

Welcome

Page 3, Exercise 2A – CD1, Track 2

A Hi. I'm looking for a job.
B What can you do?
A I can use a computer very well. I can speak English and Spanish. I can help students with their homework, and I can read to children.
B Can you write in English?
A Yes, I can.
B Can you speak Russian?
A No, I can't. But I'm going to learn.

Page 4, Exercise 3A – CD1, Track 3

1. I am a student at Preston Adult Learning Center.
2. My English classes are very interesting.
3. My classmates are from many different countries.
4. My teacher is from Canada.
5. Maria and Gricela are from Peru.
6. They were in my class last semester, too.
7. The teacher was Ms. Gonzalez.

Page 4, Exercise 3B – CD1, Track 4

My name is Maria. I am from Mexico. My husband's name is Sergio. He's from Mexico, too. There are three children in our family – one son and two daughters. Our son, Javier, is seven years old. He was born in Mexico. Our daughters, Melisa and Maritza, are twins. They are one year old. They were born in the United States. Sergio and I weren't born in the United States. We were born in Mexico.

Page 5, Exercise 4A – CD1, Track 5

1. Bao takes out the garbage every week.
2. I work at a restaurant every day.
3. Eva visited her parents in the afternoon.
4. We celebrated my parents' fiftieth anniversary last night.
5. Sarah went to the baseball game yesterday.
6. Mike took the bus last week.
7. She didn't buy candy yesterday.
8. He wants to go to the mall on Saturday.
9. Akiko sleeps late on Sundays.
10. They don't usually walk to school.

Page 5, Exercise 4B – CD1, Track 6

A When did you come to this country?
B I came here two years ago.
A You speak very well. Did you study English here last year?
B Yes, I did.
A Did you speak English in your native country?
B No, I didn't.
A What do you usually do on the weekend?
B I usually stay home, but sometimes I go shopping.

Unit 1: Personal information

Page 7, Exercises 2A and 2B – CD1, Track 7

Conversation A

A Shoko, who's this?
B This is a picture of my daughter, Victoria.
A What's she wearing?
B Her soccer uniform. She plays every day. She's very athletic.
A Wow! She's really tall.
B Yes, she is. She looks like her father.
A She's a pretty girl. Her long black hair is beautiful.

Conversation B

A Shoko, is that your son?
B Yes. This is my teenage son, Eddie.
A What's he doing?
B He's playing computer games. He always plays computer games!
A Does he have a lot of friends?
B No, not many. He's a very quiet boy.

Conversation C

B This is a picture of my husband, Mark.
A Oh, Shoko, he is tall!
B Yes, he is. He wears very large shirts and pants. I buy his clothes at a special store.
A What does he do?
B He's an engineer. He's very smart. He studies English, too.
A You have a really nice family.
B Thanks.

Page 8, Exercise 2A – CD1, Track 8

1. **A** What's Amy wearing?
   B She's wearing a long black dress.
2. **A** What's she wearing?
   B She's wearing black and white checked pants.
3. **A** What does he take to school?
   B He takes a large red backpack.
4. **A** What do you usually wear to work?
   B I wear a blue and white striped uniform.
5. **A** What's he wearing today?
   B He's wearing a red and yellow plaid sweater.
6. **A** What are they wearing?
   B They're wearing short green skirts.
7. **A** What do you like to wear at home?
   B I like to wear my long brown plaid bathrobe.
8. **A** What does she wear to the park?
   B She wears a green and white striped jogging suit.

Page 10, Exercise 2A – CD1, Track 9

1. **A** What does Ed do every night?
   B He relaxes.
   A What's Ed doing right now?
   B He's watching TV.
2. **A** What's Mary doing right now?
   B She's teaching.
   A What does Mary do every Tuesday?
   B She teaches.
3. **A** What's Isaac doing right now?
   B He's studying.
   A What does Isaac do every day?
   B He goes to class.

Page 12, Exercise 2 – CD1, Track 10

Hi Karin,

How are you doing? Guess what! Today is my daughter's birthday. The last time you saw Victoria, she was three years old. Now she's 17! She's tall and very athletic. She likes sports. She plays soccer every afternoon. Here is her photo. She's wearing her red and white striped soccer uniform. She usually wears jeans and a T-shirt. Victoria is also a very good student. She has lots of friends and goes with them to the mall every weekend. How are your daughters? Please send a photo! Let's stay in touch.

Shoko

Page 13, Exercise 4A – CD1, Track 11

1. a hat
2. a tie
3. a watch
4. sunglasses
5. a scarf
6. gloves
7. a purse
8. earrings
9. a necklace
10. a bracelet
11. a belt
12. a ring

Unit 2: At school

Page 19, Exercises 2A and 2B – CD1, Track 12

Conversation A

A Oh, what's wrong with this computer!
B Um, Joseph, do you need help?

A Oh, thanks, Eva. I'm having trouble with this keyboard. I need to take a computer class.
B Ask the teacher about keyboarding classes. She helped me find a citizenship class.
A That's a great idea. I'll talk to Mrs. Lee after class. Thanks!
B You're welcome, Joseph. Good luck!

Conversation B

C Oh, hi, Joseph. Do you need something?
A Yes, Mrs. Lee. I want to learn keyboarding skills. What do I need to do?
C Hmm . . . keyboarding skills. Do you need to use a computer at work?
A No, not right now. But someday I want to open my own business. I'm pretty sure I'll need to use a computer then.
C Well, you can study keyboarding in the computer lab across the hall. You could talk with Mr. Stephens. He's the lab instructor.
A Thanks, Mrs. Lee. I'll talk to Mr. Stephens right now.

Conversation C

A Hello, Mr. Stephens. My name is Joseph. Mrs. Lee told me to come here. I want to learn keyboarding.
D That's great. You can join my keyboarding class. First, you need to register with Mrs. Smith in the Registration Office.
A Great. I'll go register now.
D But there's one problem.
A One problem?
D Yes. The Registration Office is closed today. You can register next week.
A OK. Thanks.

Page 20, Exercise 2A – CD1, Track 13

1. A What do you want to do now?
   B I want to get my GED.
2. A What do you need to do?
   B I need to take a GED class.
3. A What does Sandra want to do this year?
   B She wants to learn about computers.
4. A What do the students need to buy?
   B They need to buy a student ID card.
5. A What does Ali want to do this year?
   B He wants to make more money.
6. A What does Celia need to do tonight?
   B She needs to do her homework.
7. A What do Sergio and Elena want to do next year?
   B They want to become citizens.
8. A What does Maria need to do?
   B She needs to make dinner.

Page 22, Exercise 2A – CD1, Track 14

1. Sue will go to her English class on Monday. She will have coffee with Ruth. She won't go to the gym.
2. Sue has a test on Wednesday. She will probably study Tuesday after work. She won't go to Emily's party.
3. On Wednesday, she will go to her English class, and she will go to the gym. Maybe she will have coffee with Ruth.
4. She probably won't go to the movie with Jose on Thursday. She will be too tired after work.
5. Sue will go to the gym on Friday, and she will most likely go to the movie with Jose.
6. On Saturday, Sue will write her English paragraph. She probably won't go to her Salsa dance lesson. She will go to the family birthday party.

Page 24, Exercise 2 – CD1, Track 15

What are your future goals? What steps do you need to take?
I want to open my own electronics store. I need to take three steps to reach my goal. First, I need to learn keyboarding. Second, I need to take business classes. Third, I need to work in an electronics store. I will probably open my store in a couple of years.

Page 25, Exercise 4A – CD1, Track 16

1. home health care
2. counseling
3. small engine repair
4. physical therapy
5. criminal justice
6. fitness training
7. hotel management
8. accounting
9. computer networking

Review: Units 1 and 2

Page 30, Exercise 1 – CD1, Track 17

Fernando Reyes is thirty-five years old. He's from Colombia. He's tall and has curly brown hair and green eyes. Fernando has a very busy schedule. He goes to school in the morning. After school, he works at Green's Grocery Store from 1 to 9. He's a cashier there. He usually plays soccer with his friends on Saturday. Fernando wants to study computer technology. He needs to take classes at the community college. Next month, he'll begin computer classes.

Page 31, Exercise 3A – CD1, Track 18

paper
restaurant
computer

Page 31, Exercise 3B – CD1, Track 19

necklace	counselor
keyboard	uniform
bracelet	manager
sweater	citizen
jacket	mechanic
cashier	tomorrow
career	computer
repair	eraser
achieve	television
medium	citizenship

Page 31, Exercise 3C – CD1, Track 20

1. instructor
2. partner
3. enroll
4. dictionary
5. business
6. sunglasses
7. management
8. relax
9. important

Unit 3: Friends and family

Page 33, Exercises 2A and 2B – CD1, Track 21

Conversation A

A Rigatoni Restaurant. Daniel speaking.
B Hi, Daniel? It's me.
A Rosa? Hi. Is everything OK?
B Not really. I went to the supermarket with the children, and the car broke down.
A The car broke down! What's wrong?
B I don't know. I think it's the engine.
A Did you open the hood?
B Yes, I did. There's a lot of smoke!
A Where are you?
B I'm at the side of the road near the supermarket.
A Stay there. I'm going to leave work right now. I'll be there in ten minutes.
B OK. I have a lot of groceries in the trunk. Please hurry.

Conversation B

C Mike's Auto Repair.
B Hi, Mike, It's Rosa – Daniel's wife?
C Oh, hi, Rosa. How are you?
B Well, not so good.
C Why? What's wrong?
B Well, this morning I went to the store to buy groceries for a picnic, but then our car broke down. My husband came and picked us up.
C Oh, I'm sorry, Rosa.
B Could you pick up the car for us? It's on the side of the road near the supermarket.

C Of course. I'll pick it up and take it to my shop this afternoon.
B Thanks, Mike.

Conversation C
D Hello, Swift Dry Cleaner's.
B Hi, Ling. It's Rosa. How are you?
D I'm good. I'm almost done with work. Will I see you tonight?
B I'm not sure. We had car trouble today. I need a ride to school tonight. Can you pick me up?
D Sure. What time?
B I usually leave my house at 7 o'clock.
D Ok. I'll pick you up at 7.
B That's great. You're a good friend, Ling. Thank you.
D No problem. See you tonight.

Page 34, Exercise 2A – CD1, Track 22

1. **A** What did Dahlia and her friends do on Sunday?
   B They grilled hamburgers.
2. **A** What did the children do on Thursday?
   B They took a walk in the park.
3. **A** What did your family do last weekend?
   B We drove to the beach.
4. **A** What did Sarah do Monday night?
   B She went to the movies.
5. **A** What did Nikos do Saturday morning?
   B He fixed the car.
6. **A** Did Carlos buy groceries yesterday?
   B No, he didn't.
7. **A** Did Ana study last night?
   B Yes, she did.
8. **A** Did Pedro meet his friend at the airport last Saturday?
   B No, he didn't.
9. **A** Did the Lopez family have a party at their house last weekend?
   B Yes, they did.
10. **A** Did Maria and her husband play cards on Friday night?
    B No, they didn't.

Page 36, Exercise 2A – CD1, Track 23

1. **A** When does Sharon usually meet her friends?
   B She usually meets her friends after work.
   A When did Sharon meet her friends yesterday?
   B Yesterday, she met them at noon for lunch.
2. **A** What time do Roberto and Selma usually eat dinner?
   B They usually eat dinner at 7 o'clock.
   A When did they eat dinner last night?
   B They ate dinner at 8 o'clock.
3. **A** When do Irma and Ron usually study?
   B They usually study on Saturday.
   A When did they study last weekend?
   B They studied on Friday night.
4. **A** When do you usually watch movies?
   B I usually watch movies after dinner.
   A What time did you watch a movie last night?
   B I watched a movie at 6 o'clock.

Page 38, Exercise 2 – CD1, Track 24

Thursday, June 20th
Today was a bad day! On Thursday, my children and I usually go to the park for a picnic, but today we had a problem. We drove to the store to buy groceries, and then the car broke down. I checked the engine, and there was a lot of smoke. I think the engine overheated. Luckily, I had my cell phone! First, I called my husband at work. He left early, picked us up, and took us home. Next, I called the mechanic. Finally, I called Ling and asked for a ride to school tonight. In the end, we didn't go to the park because it was too late. Instead, we had a picnic in our backyard. Then, Ling drove me to school.

Page 39, Exercise 4A – CD1, Track 25

1. make lunch
2. take a bath
3. do the dishes
4. do the laundry
5. get up
6. do homework
7. take a nap
8. make the bed
9. get dressed

Unit 4: Health

Page 45, Exercises 2A and 2B – CD1, Track 26

Conversation A
A Hello?
B Lily, it's me. I had a little accident.
A Are you OK, Hamid? What happened?
B I fell off a ladder at work. I hurt my leg.
A Hamid, you should go to the hospital!
B I'm at the hospital now. But listen, you have to pick up the children at school. I have to wait for the doctor.
A OK, I'll pick up the children. I'll see you back at home.
B OK, thanks, Lily. Bye.

Conversation B
C Hello?
B Chris, it's Hamid.
C Hey, how's it going?
B Not so good. I had a little accident at work. I fell off a ladder.
C Oh, no. Are you OK?
B Well, I hurt my leg. I'm at the hospital now, and I had to get an X-ray. Could you come to the hospital and drive me home?
C Of course. What's the address?
B It's 3560 East 54th Street. You should take the highway.
C OK, I'm leaving right now.
B Thanks, Chris. Bye.

Conversation C
D Ace Construction.
B Hi, Angie. It's Hamid. I need to talk to Mr. Jackson, please.
D Hi, Hamid. Just a second.
E Hi, Hamid. Jackson here. How's it going? Did you finish painting the house on Main Street?
B Well, no. I had a little accident. I slipped and fell off the ladder. I'm at the hospital now.
E Oh, no! Are you badly hurt?
B I don't know. I had to get an X-ray of my leg. The doctor is looking at the X-ray now.
E Hamid, you have to fill out an accident report. Call me after you see the doctor.
B OK. What about the paint job?
E Don't worry. Felipe will finish it. Stay home tomorrow. You should rest.
B OK. Thanks, Mr. Jackson. Bye.

Page 46, Exercise 2A – CD1, Track 27

1. **A** Ken's eyes hurt. What should he do?
   B He should rest. He shouldn't read right now.
2. **A** They have stomachaches. What should they do?
   B They shouldn't eat. They should take some medicine.
3. **A** My tooth hurts. What should I do?
   B You should see a dentist.
4. **A** Mia has a headache. What should she do?
   B She should take some aspirin.
5. **A** I hurt my leg. What should I do?
   B You should get an X-ray. You shouldn't walk.
6. **A** I have a bottle of medicine. What should I do?
   B You should read the label. You shouldn't keep it in a hot place.
7. **A** We are very tired. What should we do?
   B We should rest. We shouldn't work so hard.

Page 48, Exercise 2A – CD1, Track 28

1. **A** Elian hurt his leg.
   B He has to get an X-ray.
2. **A** Kathy and Tom have asthma.
   B They have to take their medicine.
3. **A** Are your eyes bad?
   B Yes, they are. I have to wear glasses.
4. **A** Marcia has a sprained ankle.
   B She has to get a pair of crutches.
5. **A** Nick and Tony had an accident at work.
   B They have to fill out an accident report.
6. **A** Pam hurt her back.
   B She has to go home early.
7. **A** Do you have asthma?
   B Yes, I do. I have to use an inhaler.
8. **A** My son broke his arm.
   B You have to take him to the hospital.

Page 50, Exercise 2 – CD1, Track 29

WARNING: PREVENT ACCIDENTS.
READ BEFORE USING!
Face the ladder when climbing up and down.
Don't carry a lot of equipment while climbing a ladder – wear a tool belt.
Never stand on the shelf of the ladder – stand on the steps.
Never stand on the top step of a ladder.
Be safe! Always read and follow the safety stickers.

Page 51, Exercise 4A – CD1, Track 30

1. a swollen knee
2. a sprained wrist
3. chest pains
4. high blood pressure
5. allergies
6. chills
7. a bad cut
8. a rash
9. a stiff neck

Review: Units 3 and 4

Page 56, Exercise 1 – CD1, Track 31

Trinh is a nurse. She works Monday to Friday at City Children's Hospital. On the weekend, she and her family usually stay home. But this was a special weekend for Trinh.
On Friday morning, she and her husband became citizens. In the afternoon, they went to a restaurant. On Saturday, they took their son and daughter to the beach. The children played all day. Trinh and her husband read and took pictures of the children. In the evening, they grilled hamburgers with some friends. Then they went home and watched a movie. Trinh is happy to be a citizen and happy that her family had a good time.

Page 57, Exercise 3A – CD1, Track 32

Tina's car broke down.
Oscar has to take his medicine.

Page 57, Exercise 3B – CD1, Track 33

1. His wife had to do it.
2. Van has a headache.
3. I played soccer last night.
4. They went to the library yesterday.
5. Eliza works in the afternoon.
6. Sam made breakfast.

Page 57, Exercise 3C – CD1, Track 34

1. Ali cut his arm.
2. He went to the hospital.
3. His sister took him.
4. He saw the doctor.
5. He has to take some medicine.
6. He shouldn't carry heavy items.

Unit 5: Around town

Page 59, Exercises 2A and 2B – CD1, Track 35

Conversation A

A Attention, please. This is an announcement.
B What's that, Binh?
C That's just an announcement, Mom. The announcer is giving train information. We should listen.
A Trains to Boston leave every hour. The next train to Boston will leave at 7:20 from Track 1.
I repeat. The next train to Boston will leave at 7:20 from Track 1.
B That was about trains to Boston. We need information about trains to New York.
C Wait. Here's another announcement.
A Trains to New York City leave every . . . The next train to New York will leave at . . . I repeat. The next train to New York will leave at . . . from Track 2.
B Oh, no! We didn't hear the information about New York!

Conversation B

B There's an information desk over there. You can ask about trains from Philadelphia to New York.
C Oh, good. Excuse me. I need some train information.
D How can I help you?
C I'm taking my mother to New York City today. How often do trains go to New York?
D Trains leave for New York every 30 minutes.
C When does the next train leave for New York?
D The 7:05 train just left. The next train leaves at 7:35 from Track 3.
C Thanks.
D Do you have tickets? You can get them at the ticket booth over there.
C No, we don't have tickets. Thank you very much.

Conversation C

C I got our tickets, Mom. Our train leaves in 25 minutes.
B Good. We don't have to wait long.
C Do you want to sit down? We can sit in the waiting area.
B That's a good idea. My suitcase is heavy. This train station is beautiful.
C Yeah, it really is. I always travel by train. It's a lot easier than driving.
B How long does it take to drive to New York?
C It usually takes about 2 hours to drive. It takes less than one and a half hours by train.
A Attention, please. The train to New York is now boarding on Track 3.
C That's our train, Mom. Let's go!

Page 60, Exercise 2A – CD1, Track 36

1. **A** How often does Binh go to New York?
   B Twice a month.
2. **A** How long does it take to fly to Mexico?
   B A long time.
3. **A** How often do you study?
   B Twice a week.
4. **A** How long does it take to drive to Toronto?
   B Seven hours.
5. **A** How long does it take to walk to school?
   B 20 minutes.
6. **A** How often does Sandra cook dinner?
   B Three times a week.
7. **A** How often does the bus go to Springfield?
   B Once a day.
8. **A** How often do they go on vacation?
   B Once a year.
9. **A** How long does it take to drive to the airport?
   B One hour.
10. **A** How long does it take to walk to the library?
    B 25 minutes.

Page 62, Exercise 2A – CD1, Track 37

1. Teresa always drives to work in the morning.
2. She is rarely late.
3. Her husband usually walks to work.
4. He sometimes takes a taxi.
5. He never drives
6. Their daughter always rides her bike to school.
7. She is often tired in the morning.
8. Her daughter is rarely absent from school.
9. Teresa never goes to the library on Sunday.
10. Her husband is hardly ever sick.

Page 64, Exercise 2 – CD1, Track 38

Hi Layla,

Right now, my mother is visiting me here in Philadelphia. I rarely see her because she comes to Philadelphia only once a year. She usually stays for one month. Here is a photo of my mother at the airport last week. She was happy to see me!
This year, I want to take my mother to New York City. I want to show her the Statue of Liberty and Central Park. It takes about one and a half hours to get to New York by train. We are excited about our trip. Can you meet us there? I'm thinking about the end of March. Let me know.
Can't wait to see you!
Write me soon.

Binh

Page 65, Exercise 4A – CD1, Track 39

1. write postcards
2. stay at a hotel
3. take a suitcase
4. buy souvenirs
5. go swimming
6. stay with relatives
7. take pictures
8. go shopping
9. go sightseeing

Unit 6: Time

Page 71, Exercises 2A and 2B – CD2, Track 2

Conversation A

A Olga, I love your new apartment.
B Thanks, Victoria. We moved in two months ago. You're our first visitor.
A Is that your wedding picture?
B Yes, it is. That's my husband and me a long time ago.
A What a good-looking bride and groom! When did you get married?
B Let's see. We got married in 1999.
A You were young! My husband and I had our third wedding anniversary last month. Do you have more pictures?
B Sure. They're in our photo album. Do you want to see them?
A I'd love to.

Conversation B

A Your pictures are wonderful. You have a lovely family.
B Thanks!
A How old are your children?
B My son, Sergey, is 18 now. His birthday was three days ago. He started college in September.
A When did your daughter start college?
B Start college? Natalya's only 14!
A Wow! She's tall for her age.
B Yes, she is. She started high school on Tuesday.

Conversation C

A Is that a picture of Russia?
B Yes. That's in Moscow.
A Did you live in Moscow?
B Yes. We met in Moscow. We went to school there before we got married.
A It looks like an interesting city.
B Oh, it is!
A When did you move to the United States?
B We moved here about 14 years ago.
A Were your children born here?
B Natalya was. Sergey was born in Russia, like us.

Page 72, Exercise 2A – CD2, Track 3

1. **A** When did Min leave South Korea?
   B She left South Korea in 2014.
   A When did she move to New York?
   B She moved to New York in 2016.
2. **A** When did Carlos start school?
   B He started school in September.
   A When did he graduate?
   B He graduated in June.
3. **A** When did Paul and Amy meet?
   B They met in 2014.
   A When did they get married?
   B They got married in 2017.
4. **A** When did you finish college?
   B I finished college in August.
   A When did you get your first job?
   B I got my first job in September.

Page 74, Exercise 2A – CD2, Track 4

1. **A** When did Lou and Angela buy their new car?
   B They bought their new car three weeks ago.
2. **A** When did Lou and Angela get married?
   B They got married four years ago.
3. **A** When did Angela have a baby?
   B She had a baby yesterday at 8:20 a.m.
4. **A** When did Lou begin his new job?
   B He began his new job on Tuesday.
5. **A** When did Lou move to the United States?
   B He moved to the United States on December 15th.
6. **A** When did Angela come to the United States?
   B She came to the United States five years ago.
7. **A** When did Angela take the citizenship exam?
   B She took the citizenship exam in March.
8. **A** When did Angela register to vote?
   B She registered to vote in June.

Page 76, Exercise 2 – CD2, Track 5

An Interesting Life
Interviewer: What happened after you graduated from high school?
Olga: I went to university in Moscow, and I met my husband there. It was a long time ago! We were in the same class. We fell in love and got married on April 2nd, 1999. We had a small wedding in Moscow.
Interviewer: What happened after you got married?
Olga: I finished university and found a job. I was a teacher. Then, I had a baby. My husband and I were very excited to have a little boy.
Interviewer: When did you move to the United States?
Olga: We immigrated about 14 years ago. We became American citizens eight years ago.

Page 77, Exercise 4A – CD2, Track 6

1. retired
2. started a business
3. had a baby
4. fell in love
5. got engaged
6. got married
7. got divorced
8. immigrated
9. got promoted

Review: Units 5 and 6

Page 82, Exercise 1 – CD2, Track 7

A Flight 464 to Denver will begin boarding in five minutes at Gate 3C. Passengers should be at the gate at this time.
B Marie! What are you doing here?
C I just came back from Florida. My parents live there now.
B How nice. How often do you see them?
C I go there every three months. So, what are you doing here?

B I'm meeting my brother, David. He always comes here for his vacation. He stays for about a week. Then he goes to Texas to visit our sister.
A Flight 783 from Atlanta is now arriving at Gate 32.
B Well, that's David's flight. I need to go. Good to see you.
C You, too. Have fun with your brother.

Page 83, Exercise 3A – CD2, Track 8

Where is the train station?
Is the train station on Broadway or on Main Street?

Page 83, Exercise 3B – CD2, Track 9

Wh- questions
A How often do you eat at a restaurant?
B Once a week.

***Or* questions**
A Do you eat at a restaurant once a week or once a month?
B Once a week.

Unit 7: Shopping

Page 85, Exercises 2A and 2B – CD2, Track 10

Conversation A
A Good afternoon, folks. I'm Mike. How can I help you?
B Hi, I'm Denise. This is my husband, Nick. We need some furniture.
C A lot of furniture!
B We bought a house two days ago.
A Congratulations! This is the right place for furniture and appliances. We're having our biggest sale of the year. All our furniture is marked down 20 percent.
B Wow! 20 percent.
A We have chairs, lamps, sofas. . . . Look around. We have the best prices in town.
B Are the appliances 20 percent off, too?
A Yes! Refrigerators, stoves – everything in the store is 20 percent off.
C Thanks.

Conversation B
B Nick, look at that sofa. It's very pretty!
C Which one? The brown one?
B No, not the brown one, the blue one. It looks nice and comfortable. I like it.
C Hmm. But the brown sofa is bigger. I want a big sofa.
B Well, it is bigger, but look at the price, Nick. It's much more expensive than the blue sofa.
C Whoa! A thousand dollars? That's crazy!
B Look, there are some more sofas over there. Maybe they're cheaper.
C I sure hope so.

Conversation C
B Oh, look, Nick. They have pianos for sale.
C Pianos? But we aren't looking for a piano. We're looking for a sofa.
B I love this piano. Excuse me, miss? Do you work here?
D Yes. My name is Tara. How can I help you?
B Could you tell me about this piano?
D Oh, the upright piano? It's very old, but it's the most beautiful piano in the store. It also has a beautiful sound. Listen.
B Wow! Is it expensive?
D Well, it's $960. This small piano is cheaper, but the sound isn't the same.
B The upright piano is better. Let's buy it, Nick!
C Hey, not so fast! We came here to buy a sofa, not a piano!

Page 86, Exercise 2A – CD2, Track 11

1. **A** Which chair is heavier?
   B The orange chair is heavier.
2. **A** Which refrigerator is more expensive?
   B The large refrigerator is more expensive.
3. **A** Which table is bigger?
   B The square table is bigger.
4. **A** Which stove is better?
   B The black stove is better.
5. **A** Which lamp is taller?
   B The floor lamp is taller.
6. **A** Which sofa is more comfortable?
   B The green striped sofa is more comfortable.

Page 88, Exercise 2A – CD2, Track 12

1. **A** Which TV is the cheapest?
   B The second TV is the cheapest.
2. **A** Which TV is the heaviest?
   B The second TV is the heaviest.
3. **A** Which TV is the most expensive?
   B The first TV is the most expensive.
4. **A** Which TV is the oldest?
   B The second TV is the oldest.
5. **A** Which TV is the smallest?
   B The third TV is the smallest.
6. **A** Which TV is the biggest?
   B The first TV is the biggest.
7. **A** Which TV is the best.
   B The first TV is the best.
8. **A** Which TV is the newest?
   B The first TV is the newest.

Page 89, Exercise 2B – CD2, Track 13

A This is the newest shopping mall in the city. It's great.
B Where's the best place to buy clothes?
A Well, there are three clothing stores. Mega Store is the biggest one. It usually has the lowest prices, but it's the most crowded. I never go there.
B What about Cleo's Boutique?
A Cleo's Boutique is the most beautiful store. It's nice, but it's the most expensive.
B What about Madison's?
A Well, it's the smallest, but it's my favorite. It has the nicest clothes and the friendliest salespeople.
B Look! Madison's is having a big sale. Let's go!

Page 90, Exercise 2 – CD2, Track 14

Today's Question
What's the best thing you ever bought?
The best thing I ever bought was an old piano. I bought it in a used-furniture store last month. It was the most beautiful piano in the store, but it wasn't very expensive. It has a beautiful sound. Now my two children are taking piano lessons. I love to hear music in the house.
Denise Robinson – Charleston, South Carolina
I bought a used van five years ago. I used my van to help people move and to deliver stoves and refrigerators from a secondhand appliance store. I made a lot of money with that van. Now I have my own business. That van is the best thing I ever bought.
Sammy Chin – Myrtle Beach, South Carolina

Page 91, Exercise 4A – CD2, Track 15

1. aquarium
2. computer desk
3. mirror
4. end table
5. sofa bed
6. bookcase
7. entertainment center
8. coffee table
9. recliner

Unit 8: Work

Page 97, Exercises 2A and 2B – CD2, Track 16

Conversation A
A Hey, Marco. How are you?
B Oh, hi, Arlen. I'm fine. I had a busy day today.
A What did you do?

B Hmm . . . let's see. This morning, I delivered flowers to patients and picked up X-rays from the lab. I also delivered clean linens to the third floor. This afternoon, I made the beds on the second floor and prepared the rooms. And now I'm delivering supplies.

A Wow! You did have a busy day!

Conversation B

B Hi, John. How's it going?

C Hi, Marco. I'm tired. I worked the night shift last night.

B Oh, no.

C I like this job, but I don't like the night shift.

B I like this job, too, but I don't like the pay. I'm thinking about going back to school.

C Really? School is expensive.

B I know. Maybe I can find a part-time job and go to school full-time.

C Maybe you can work here part-time. You should ask about it.

Conversation C

B Is this the HR Office? Human Resources?

D Yes, come on in. I'm Suzanne Briggs. I'm the HR Assistant.

B Hi, Suzanne. I'm Marco Alba. I'm an orderly here.

D Hi, Marco. Have a seat. How can I help you?

B I like my job here, but I don't want to be an orderly forever. I want to go to nursing school and become a nurse.

D A nurse? That's great, Marco!

B I want to go to nursing school full-time and work part-time.

D That's a great idea! A lot of employees do that.

B Can I work part-time here at Valley Hospital?

D I don't know. Can you come back tomorrow? I'll find out about part-time jobs for you.

B Sure. Thanks, Suzanne. See you tomorrow.

Page 98, Exercise 2A – CD2, Track 17

1. **A** What did Linda do after breakfast?
   B She made the beds.
2. **A** What did Brenda and Leo do this morning?
   B They picked up patients in the reception area.
3. **A** What did Trevor do this morning?
   B He delivered X-rays.
4. **A** Where did Jill and Brad take the linens?
   B They took the linens to the second floor.
5. **A** What did Felix do yesterday?
   B He helped patients with their walkers and wheelchairs.
6. **A** Where did Juan and Ivana go after work?
   B They went to the coffee shop across the street.
7. **A** What did Marco do after lunch?
   B He prepared the rooms on the 2nd floor.
8. **A** Where did Suzanne meet Marco?
   B She met him in her office.

Page 100, Exercise 2A – CD2, Track 18

1. Sometimes Irene eats Chinese food for lunch. Sometimes she eats Mexican food for Lunch. Irene eats Chinese or Mexican food for lunch.
2. Tito works the day shift. Tito also works the night shift. Tito works the day shift and the night shift.
3. Marco had an interview. He didn't get the job. Marco had an interview, but he didn't get the job.
4. Brian likes his co-workers. He doesn't like his schedule. Brian likes his co-workers, but he doesn't like his schedule.
5. Erica takes care of her children. She also takes care of her grandmother. Erica takes care of her children and her grandmother.
6. Carl cleaned the carpets. He didn't make the beds. Carl cleaned the carpets, but he didn't make the beds.
7. Sometimes Kate works in Austin. Sometimes she works in Houston. Kate works in Austin or in Houston.
8. Ilya speaks Russian at home. He also speaks Russian at work. Ilya speaks Russian at home and at work.

Page 102, Exercise 2 – CD2, Track 19

Dear Mr. O'Hara:
I am happy to write this recommendation for Marco Alba. Marco started working at Valley Hospital as an orderly in 2016. He takes patients from their rooms to the lab, delivers X-rays, and takes flowers and mail to patients. He also delivers linens and supplies. He is an excellent worker, and his co-workers like him very much.
We are sorry to lose Marco. He wants to go to school and needs to work part-time, but we don't have a part-time job for him right now. I recommend Marco very highly. Please contact me for more information.
Sincerely,
Suzanne Briggs
Human Resources Assistant

Page 103, Exercise 4A – CD2, Track 20

1. repair cars
2. operate large machines
3. clear tables
4. prepare food
5. help the nurses
6. take care of a family
7. handle money
8. assist the pharmacist
9. assist the doctor

Review: Units 7 and 8

Page 108, Exercise 1 – CD2, Track 21

Yuri works part-time at Furniture Mart. He's a salesperson. He talks to customers and helps them find good furniture at low prices. He likes his job. Yesterday, Yuri met Mr. and Mrs. Chan at the store. They wanted a new sofa and an entertainment center. Their old sofa wasn't comfortable. They looked at two sofas. The first sofa was $599. It was nice, but it wasn't very big. The second sofa was more expensive. It was $749. It was more comfortable, and it was bigger, too. The Chans bought the second sofa and two lamps, but they didn't buy the entertainment center. After work, Yuri ate dinner at China House Restaurant. Mr. Chan is the manager there.

Page 109, Exercise 3A – CD2, Track 22

/d/
used: She used the new machine.
delivered: You delivered the mail.

/t/
helped: He helped the nurses.
worked: He worked on the weekends.

/id/
wanted: They wanted to make the beds.
assisted: She assisted the patient.

Page 109, Exercise 3B – CD2, Track 23

/id/
repaired
prepared
played

/t/
picked
cooked
walked

/id/
needed
started
visited

Page 109, Exercise 3C – CD2, Track 24

1. cleaned
2. operated
3. finished
4. handled
5. pushed
6. checked
7. answered
8. reported

Unit 9: Daily living

Page 111, Exercises 2A and 2B – CD2, Track 25

Conversation A

A Hello, Building Manager.
B Hi, this is Stella Taylor in Apartment 4B. I've got a problem. The washing machine overflowed. And the dishwasher's leaking, too. And the sink is clogged. Could you please recommend a plumber?
A Well, I usually use two different plumbers.
B Which one do you recommend?
A Let's see. His name is Don Brown. He has a company on Main Street. Here's the phone number: 555-4564. He's really good.
B Thanks. I'll call him right away.

Conversation B

C Brown's Plumbing Service, Martha speaking. May I help you?
B I hope so. My washing machine overflowed, and my dishwasher is leaking all over the floor, and my sink is clogged. May I speak to Don Brown, please?
C Oh, Don's out right now on a job. But he'll be finished in an hour. He can come then. Can you wait an hour?
B One hour? Hmm. I need to go to work soon. Maybe my neighbor can unlock the door for him. My address is 3914 Fifth Street, Apartment 4B.
C OK. He'll be there in an hour.
B Thank you.

Conversation C

D Russell Taylor speaking.
B Hi, Russell. It's me. I have bad news. The washing machine overflowed, and the dishwasher is leaking on the floor, and the sink is clogged!
D Oh, no. Look, I'm really busy at work right now. Could you please call a plumber?
B I already did.
D You did? Which plumber did you call?
B Brown's Plumbing Service. The plumber will be here in an hour.
D But you're going to work.
B It's OK. I asked Mrs. Lee to let him in.
D All right, Stella. I'll see you tonight.

Page 112, Exercise 2A – CD2, Track 26

1. **A** Could you fix the dryer, please?
   B Yes, of course.
2. **A** Can you unclog the sink, please?
   B No, not now. Maybe later.
3. **A** Would you clean the carpet, please?
   B Sorry, I can't right now.
4. **A** Will you repair the oven?
   B Sure, I'd be happy to.
5. **A** Will you fix the lock, please?
   B No, not now. Maybe later.
6. **A** Could you fix the window, please?
   B Yes, of course.
7. **A** Would you repair the dishwasher, please?
   B Sure. I'd be happy to.
8. **A** Can you change the light bulb?
   B Sorry, I can't right now.

Page 114, Exercise 2A – CD2, Track 27

1. **A** Which plumbing service do you recommend – Harrison's or Brown's?
   B I recommend Brown's Plumbing Service because it's cheaper.
2. **A** Which plumbing service does he recommend – Harrison's or Brown's?
   B He recommends Harrison's Plumbing Service because it's fast.
3. **A** Which plumbing service do they recommend – Harrison's or Brown's?
   B They recommend Brown's Plumbing Service because it's licensed.
4. **A** Which plumbing service does she recommend – Harrison's or Brown's?
   B She recommends Brown's Plumbing Service because it's insured.
5. **A** Which plumbing service do they recommend – Harrison's or Brown's?
   B They recommend Harrison's Plumbing Service because it's more experienced.
6. **A** Which plumbing service does he recommend – Harrison's or Brown's?
   B He recommends Harrison's Plumbing Service because it's open 24 hours a day.

Page 116, Exercise 2 – CD2, Track 28

Attention, tenants:
Do you have problems in your apartment?
Is anyone fixing them?
Many tenants have broken windows.
Tenants on the third floor have no lights in the hall.
A tenant on the second floor has a leaking ceiling.
Tenants on the first floor smell garbage every day.
I'm really upset! We need to get together and write a letter of complaint to the manager of the building.
Come to a meeting Friday night at 7 p.m. in Apartment 4B.
Stella Taylor, Tenant 4B

Pae 117, Exercise 4A – CD2, Track 29

1. broken
2. dripping
3. torn
4. scratched
5. bent
6. burned out
7. cracked
8. stained
9. jammed

Unit 10: Free time

Page 123, Exercises 2A and 2B – CD2, Track 30

Conversation A

A Aunt Ana! Hello!
B Hi, Celia. Congratulations on your graduation! This is a wonderful party!
A Thank you for coming. Would you like some cake? My mother made it.
B I'd love some. I'm very hungry.
A Would you like something to drink?
B No, thanks. Here. I brought you some flowers. They're from my garden.
A Red roses! They're beautiful! Thank you.

Conversation B

A Hello, Mrs. Campbell. Thank you for coming to my party.
C Celia, I'm so proud of you. You were my best student. You started English class three years ago, and now you have your GED! You worked very hard.
A Thank you, Mrs. Campbell. You helped me a lot.
C Here. I brought you a card.
A Oh, thank you! Oh, that's so nice. Thank you, Mrs. Campbell.
C You're welcome.
A Come and join the party. Would you like a piece of cake?
C Yes, please. I'd love some.

Conversation C

A Hi, Sue. Thanks for coming. Where are your children?
D They're with my mother, so I can't stay long. I just wanted to congratulate you.
A Thank you. Would you like a piece of cake?
D No, thanks. I'm not hungry.
A Would you like something to drink?
D I'd love some water.
A OK. I'll get you some.

D Wait. I brought you a little present.
A Oh, thank you! Oh, Sue! My favorite perfume! Thank you!
D You're welcome. It's from our family.
A That's so nice. Please take some balloons home for your children.
D Thanks. They love balloons.

Page 124, Exercise 2A – CD2, Track 31

1. **A** Would you like a cup of coffee?
   B Yes, I would.
2. **A** Would she like some ice cream?
   B Yes, she would.
3. **A** Would they like some salad?
   B Yes, they would.
4. **A** Would he like a hot dog?
   B No, thank you. He just ate one.
5. **A** Would you like some cake?
   B No, thank you. I am not hungry.
6. **A** What would she like?
   B She'd like a balloon.
7. **A** What would you like?
   B I'd like a sandwich.
8. **A** What would they like?
   B They'd like some tea.
9. **A** What would he like?
   B He'd like some water.
10. **A** What would she like?
    B She'd like rice and chicken.

Page 126, Exercise 2A – CD2, Track 32

1. **A** What did Joe buy Sylvia?
   B Joe bought her flowers.
2. **A** What did Joe buy Nick?
   B Joe bought him a card.
3. **A** What did Joe write Pam?
   B Joe wrote her a letter.
4. **A** What did Joe buy Mary and Judy?
   B Joe bought them a cake.
5. **A** What did Joe give Eva?
   B Joe gave her roses.
6. **A** What did Joe send Paul?
   B Joe sent him an invitation
7. **A** What did Joe send David?
   B Joe sent him some money.
8. **A** What did Joe give Sue?
   B Joe gave her a ride.

Page 128, Exercise 2 – CD2, Track 33

I had a graduation party last Friday. My husband sent invitations to my teacher and to my relatives and friends. They all came to the party! My teacher, Mrs. Campbell, gave me a card. Some guests brought gifts for me. My Aunt Ana brought me flowers. My friend Sue gave me some perfume. My classmate, Ruth, brought me some cookies. After the party, I wrote them thank-you notes. Tomorrow, I'm going to mail the thank-you notes at the post office.

Page 129, Exercise 4A – CD2, Track 34

1. Thanksgiving
2. Independence Day
3. a wedding
4. a housewarming
5. New Year's Eve
6. Mother's Day
7. Halloween
8. a baby shower
9. Valentine's Day

Review: Units 9 and 10

Page 134, Exercise 1 – CD2, Track 35

A Did you move to your new apartment yet, Ramona?
B Yes, I moved last week. And I want to have a party to celebrate. I hope you'll come, Fabio.
A Sure. When is it?
B I don't know. Maybe next month.
A Next month? Why are you waiting so long?
B Well, my apartment is really nice, but it isn't ready yet. I want to paint the rooms. Do you know any good painters?
A Yes, I know two good painters.
B Which one do you recommend?
A Well, the first painter is Walter Hewitt. He's good, but very expensive. The second painter is free. I recommend the second one.
B The second painter is free?
A Yes, because I'm the second painter. I'm very good, and you don't have to pay me. What do you think?
B That's great. You're a good friend, Fabio!

Page 135, Exercise 3A – CD2, Track 36

/s/
talks
makes

/z/
is
has

/iz/
watches
fixes

Page 135, Exercise 3B – CD2, Track 37

/s/
wants
suggests
unlocks
/z/
prefers
recommends
does

/iz/
relaxes
teaches
scratches

Page 135, Exercise 3C – CD2, Track 38

1. drives
2. gets
3. goes
4. uses
5. takes
6. wishes
7. sleeps
8. needs

ACKNOWLEDGEMENTS

The authors and publishers acknowledge the following sources of copyright material and are grateful for the permissions granted. While every effort has been made, it has not always been possible to identify the sources of all the material used, or to trace all copyright holders. If any omissions are brought to our notice, we will be happy to include the appropriate acknowledgements on reprinting and in the next update to the digital edition, as applicable.

Key: C = Centre, T = Top, B = Below, L = Left, R = Right.

Photos

All the below images are sourced from GettyImages.

p. 4: aldomurillo/E+; p. 14, p. 23 (photo 1) and p. 36: Hero Images; p. 21 (photo 1): ColorBlind Images/Blend Images/Getty Images Plus; p. 21, p. 77 (photo 2) and p. 103 (photo 3): kali9/E+; p. 21 (photo 3): Rawpixel/iStock/Getty Images Plus; p. 21 (photo 4): RuslanDashinsky/E+; p. 21 (photo 5): Jupiterimages/liquidlibrary/Getty Images Plus; p. 21 (photo 6): Hill Street Studios/Blend Images; p. 21 (photo 7): bowdenimages/iStock/Getty Images Plus; p. 21 (photo 8): kzenon/iStock/Getty Images Plus; p. 23 (photo 2): Westend61; p. 23 (photo 3): David Young-Wolff/Photographer's Choice; p. 23 (photo 4): Blend Images - Hill Street Studios/Erik Isakson/Brand X Pictures; p. 23 (photo 5): PeopleImages/E+; p. 23 (photo 6): pengpeng/iStock/Getty Images Plus; p. 23 (photo 7): Comstock Images/Stockbyte; p. 23 (photo 8): Jupiterimages/Stockbyte; p. 25 (photo 1): sturti/iStock/Getty Images Plus; p. 25 (photo 2): Alina555/E+; p. 25 (photo 3): Wavebreakmedia/iStock/Getty Images Plus; p. 25 (photo 4): BSIP/Universal Images Group; p. 25 (photo 5): Darryl Estrine/UpperCut Images; p. 25 (photo 6): Satyrenko/iStock/Getty Images Plus; p. 25 (photo 7): andresr/E+; p. 25 (photo 8): Gary Burchell/Taxi; p. 25 (photo 9): Phil Boorman/The Image Bank; p. 39 (photo 1): AfricaImages/E+; p. 39 (photo 2): Elyse Lewin/Stockbyte; p. 39 (photo 3): TongRo Images Inc/TongRo Images; p. 39 (photo 4): Guido Mieth/Moment; p. 39 (photo 5): PeopleImages/DigitalVision; p. 39 (photo 6): JGI/Jamie Grill/Blend Images; p. 39 (photo 7): Media for Medical/Universal Images Group; p. 39 (photo 8): OSORIOartist/iStock/Getty Images Plus; p. 39 (photo 9): BJI/Blue Jean Images; p. 49: Brian Pieters/The Image Bank; p. 51 (photo 1): kosmos111/iStock/Getty Images Plus; p. 51 (photo 2): Manuel Faba Ortega/iStock/Getty Images Plus; p. 51 and p. 65 (photo 3): KatarzynaBialasiewicz/iStock/Getty Images Plus; p. 51 (photo 4): fatihhoca/E+; p. 51 (photo 5, photo 6): BSIP/UIG/Universal Images Group; p. 51 (photo 7): Kerstin Klaassen/Photographer's Choice RF; p. 51 (photo 8): gokhanilgaz/E+; p. 51 (photo 9): Ridofranz/iStock/Getty Images Plus; p. 61: Robert Mullan/Canopy; p. 63 (T): Katarina Premfors/arabianEye; p. 63 (B) and p. 77 (photo 3): ImagesBazaar; p. 65 (photo 1): Judith Wagner/Corbis; p. 65 (photo 2): Eric Audras/ONOKY; p. 65 (photo 4): Andrew Watson/Photolibrary; p. 65 (photo 5): Paul Bradbury/Caiaimage; p. 65 (photo 6): Image Source/Photodisc; p. 65 (photo 7): Cultura RM Exclusive/Gary John Norman/Cultura Exclusive; p. 65 (photo 8): Betsie Van Der Meer/Taxi; p. 65 (photo 9): william87/iStock/Getty Images Plus; p. 66 (T): Kristopher Houchin/EyeEm; p. 66 (B): Peter Unger/Lonely Planet Images; p. 69 (photo 1): skynesher/E+; p. 69 (photo 2): Steve Debenport/E+; p. 69 (photo 3): XiXinXing/iStock/Getty Images Plus; p. 69 (photo 4): Chris Hellier/Corbis Documentary; p. 69 (photo 5): Pacific Press/LightRocket; p. 69 (photo 6): Mike McKelvie/arabianEye; p. 73 (T): Jade/Blend Images; p. 73 (B): Shannon Fagan/Taxi; p. 74: Dangubic/iStock/Getty Images Plus; p. 77 (photo 1): John Lund/Drew Kelly/Blend Images; p. 77 (photo 4): Tara Moore/The Image Bank; p. 77 (photo 5): Daniel Grill; p. 77 (photo 6): djedzura/iStock/Getty Images Plus; p. 77 (photo 7): Brigitte Wodicka/Hemera/Getty Images Plus; p. 77 (photo 8): rikirisnandar/iStock Editorial/Getty Images Plus; p. 77 (photo 9): Gary Waters/Ikon Images; p. 78: Aping Vision/STS/Taxi; p. 87 (dining table): Firmafotografen/iStock/Getty Images Plus; p. 87 (kitchen table): Grigorev_Vladimir/iStock/Getty Images Plus; p. 87 (desk lamp): ivansmuk/iStock/Getty Images Plus; p. 87 (floor lamp): benimage/E+; p. 88 (L): Robert Daly/Caiaimage; p. 88 (C): Bet_Noire/iStock/Getty Images Plus; p. 88 (R): Dorling Kindersley; p. 92 (photo 2): 07_av/E+; p. 92 (photo 3): TommL/E+; p. 93: Ashlynne Lobdell/EyeEm; p. 103 (photo 1): Tanya Constantine/Blend Images; p. 103 (photo 2): Thomas Barwick/Stone; p. 103 (photo 4): Klaus Vedfelt/Iconica; p. 103 (photo 5): sturti/E+; p. 103 (photo 6): Moof/Cultura; p. 103 (photo 7): Photo-Biotic/Photolibrary; p. 103 (photo 8): Jupiterimages/Photolibrary; p. 103 (photo 9): Tempura/E+; p. 107 (photo 1): stevanovicigor/iStock/Getty Images Plus; p. 107 (photo 2):WilliamSherman/E+; p. 107 (photo 3): Bruce Laurance/Photographer's Choice; p. 107 (photo 4): PhotoAlto/Milena Boniek/Brand X Pictures; p. 107 (photo 5): Stephen Derr/Photographer's Choice; p. 107 (photo 6): jaochainoi/iStock/Getty Images Plus; p. 117 (photo 1): whitemay/E+; p. 117 (photo 2): nicolas_/E+; p. 117 (photo 3): fmajor/iStock/Getty Images Plus; p. 117 (photo 4): dziewul/iStock/Getty Images Plus; p. 117 (photo 5): Ali El Anizi/EyeEm; p. 117 (photo 6): Fne21/iStock/Getty Images Plus; p. 117 (photo 7): Robert Kneschke/EyeEm; p. 117 (photo 8): Peter Dazeley/Photographer's Choice; p. 117 (photo 9): Knut Schulz/Westend61; p. 124: Ken Seet/Corbis/VCG/Corbis; p. 125 (photo 1): bluestocking/E+; p. 125 (photo 2): robynmac/iStock/Getty Images Plus; p. 125 (photo 3): DNY59/iStock/Getty Images Plus; p. 125 (photo 4): ALEAIMAGE/E+; p. 125 (photo 5 & 9): julichka/E+; p. 125 (photo 6): DonNichols/E+; p. 125 (photo 7): RoyalSpirit/iStock/Getty Images Plus; p. 125 (photo 8): TheCrimsonMonkey/E+; p. 129 (photo 1): Tetra Images; p. 129 (photo 2): H. Armstrong Roberts/ClassicStock/Archive Photos; p. 129 (photo 3): Ashley Corbin-Teich/Image Source; p. 129 (photo 4): monkeybusinessimages/iStock/Getty Images Plus; p. 129 (photo 5): Morsa Images/Iconica; p. 129 (photo 6): mediaphotos/iStock/Getty Images Plus; p. 129 (photo 7): Oleksiy Maksymenko/All Canada Photos; p. 129 (photo 8): LWA/The Image Bank; p. 129 (photo 9): Yo Oura/Stockbyte.

The following images are from other libraries:

p. 92 (photo 1): Currency Images are courtesy of the Bureau of Engraving and Printing.

Illustrations

p. 2, p. 11, p. 13, p. 24, p. 37, p. 43, p. 44, p. 45, p. 46, p. 47, p. 48, p. 52, p. 58, p. 64, p. 72, p. 95, p. 112, p. 127, p. 133: QBS Learning; p. 35, p. 89, p. 112: Brad Hamann; p. 9: Chuck Gonzales; p. 17, p. 29, p. 86, p. 87, p. 88, p. 119, p. 121: Kenneth Batelman; p. 101: Lucy Truman; p. 37, p. 62, p. 75, p. 113: Monika Roe; p. 91: Ted Hammond; p. 48, p. 49: Travis Foster; p. 6, p. 7, p. 12, p. 18, p. 19, p. 32, p. 33, p. 38, p. 50, p. 59, p. 70, p. 71, p. 76, p. 84, p. 85, p. 90, p. 96, p. 97, p. 110, p. 111, p. 116, p. 122, p. 123, p. 128: Ben Kirchner.

Front cover photography by andresr/E+/Getty Images.

Audio produced by CityVox.